L. W. Aikin

Crystal Gems for the Sabbath-Gchool

Containing a Choice Collection of New Hymns and Tunes.....

L. W. Aikin

Crystal Gems for the Sabbath-Gchool
Containing a Choice Collection of New Hymns and Tunes.....

ISBN/EAN: 9783337083564

Printed in Europe, USA, Canada, Australia, Japan

Cover: Foto ©Thomas Meinert / pixelio.de

More available books at **www.hansebooks.com**

CRYSTAL GEMS

FOR THE

SABBATH-SCHOOL.

CONTAINING

A Choice Collection of New Hymns and Tunes,

SUITABLE FOR

ANNIVERSARIES, AND ALL OTHER EXERCISES OF THE SABBATH-
SCHOOL; TOGETHER WITH A FINE SELECTION OF
HYMNS FOR PRAYER AND PRAISE MEETINGS.

IN THE SEVEN CHARACTER NOTES.

WITH A CLEAR EXPLANATION OF FIRST PRINCIPLES OF MUSICAL SCIENCE.

By L. W. AIKIN.

PHILADELPHIA :

MILLER'S BIBLE AND PUBLISHING HOUSE,

1102 AND 1104 SANSOM STREET.

*The Character Notes secured for this work by special contract with the
Proprietor.*

PREFACE.

No other apology is necessary for the appearance of this work, than the increasing
demand for more of our most popular music to be published in J. B. AIKIN's SEVEN
CHARACTER NOTES, which are now so deservedly popular in this and other parts
of the country.

The elementary department is short; though full enough to lead to a clear under-
standing of first principles of the science of music, and is particularly adapted to young
learners.

The ten Time Lessons in scale exercises, are unquestionably the best for the most
rapid advancement of the student, in obtaining a practical knowledge of keeping time,
of any set of lessons ever offered to the public.

The tunes are selected from the most eminent authors in America, and are well
adapted to the sentiments of the hymns.

It will be found that "Crystal Gems," provides fully for Anniversaries, Exhibitions,
and other festivals of the Sabbath-School, as well as for Prayer and Praise Meetings.

Entered, according to Act of Congress, in the year 1875, by
EDWARD W. MILLER,
in the Office of the Librarian of Congress, at Washington, D. C.

J. M. ARMSTRONG, MUSIC TYPOGRAPHER, N. E. COR. CHESTNUT & 6TH STS., PHILA.

ELEMENTS OF MUSIC.

MUSICAL sounds may be considered in reference to their *Pitch*, *Length*, and *Force*. And upon these are founded three departments, which embrace the whole of the elementary principles of music.

Pitch regards a sound as *high* or *low*. *Length*, as *long* or *short*. *Force*, *loud* or *soft*.

FIRST DEPARTMENT.—RELATIVE PITCH.

The human voice is capable of producing seven distinct primary sounds. A repetition of the first of the series forms an octave, which lies at the foundation of the high and low sounds.

SCALE OF AN OCTAVE.

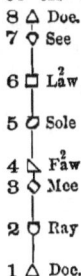

8 △ Doe.
7 ○ See

6 □ Law
2

5 ○ Sole

4 ◁ Faw
2
3 ◇ Mee

2 ○ Ray

1 △ Doe.

These notes, called *Doe*, *Ray*, *Mee*, &c., represent the eight sounds in the octave; and the spaces between the notes represent the whole and half-intervals.

The difference of pitch between two sounds is called an *interval*. Certain of these intervals are only half as great as others; hence, we have what are properly called the greater and less intervals, which, for the sake of convenience, are denominated *whole-intervals* and *half-intervals*.

The voice, in forming the scale of an octave, *naturally* rises, or falls, in whole and half-steps, or whole and half-intervals. From 1 to 2, and from 2 to 3, are whole-intervals; from 3 to 4 is a half-interval; from 4 to 5, and from 5 to 6, and from 6 to 7, are whole-intervals; and from 7 to 8 is a half-interval; making five whole-intervals, and two half-intervals in the scale of an octave. Now in addition to these sounds and intervals which the voice will *naturally* produce, we can, by an effort of the mind and organs of voice, sing intermediate sounds from 1 to 2, from 2 to 3, from 4 to 5, from 5 to 6, and from 6 to 7. These intermediate sounds are represented, in written music, by having a sharp (♯), or a flat (♭), prefixed to the note in the tune, and are called *accidental flats* and *sharps*. Thus, we say a sharp fourth (♯◁), a sharp fifth (♯○), a flat seventh (♭○), a flat third (♭◇), &c.; or, sharp *faw* (♯◁), sharp *sole* (♯○), flat *see* (♭○), flat *me* (♭◇), &c.

In singing the accidental flats and sharps, the voice is assisted in producing the proper elevation or depression by changing the pronunciation of the syllable used. Thus, when
3

a sharp occurs in a tune before *Doe, Ray, Faw,* &c., these syllables should be pronounced *Dee, Ree, Fee,* &c. When a flat occurs in a tune before *See, Mee,* &c., these syllables should be pronounced *Say, May,* &c.

RULE.—An accidental sharp (♯) elevates the pitch of a note a half-interval.

RULE.—An accidental flat (♭) depresses the pitch of a note a half-interval.

INSTRUMENTAL SOUNDS—ABSOLUTE PITCH.

Instruments furnish sounds of *absolute pitch.* Instruments are put in tune by the ear, and of course, are made to correspond with the sounds and intervals of the voice.

A is the same sound on all instruments, B is the same sound, C, and so of all the other letters. Thus, by means of instruments, we have fixed and definate sounds, so that when we speak of A, or C, or G, we speak of a sound which is known to be always and in every part of the world, the same.

The seven primary sounds on instruments, are named after the first seven letters of the alphabet. These same seven letters are located on the five lines and four spaces on the staff; so that when we find a note on A, B, or C, or any other letter on the staff, we play the corresponding or *same letter* on the instrument, which gives a definate pitch, or sounds of absolute pitch, to the notes on the staff.

A staff is five lines and four spaces as follows:

In this illustration, the lettered lines represent the sounds on the instruments, and the spaces between the lines represent the whole and half-intervals.

As there are only seven primary sounds in the science of music, it requires but the seven letters on the instrument,—which also limits seven letters on the staff.

C is called *the Natural Scale* on instruments from the fact that the instrument is based upon the *sound called C,* and requires no flats or sharps to correspond with the *natural rise* and *fall* of the voice. C is applied to the key, and is therefore 1; D is 2, E is 3, F is 4, G is 5, A is 6, B is 7, and C is 8. The half-steps or half-intervals on all instruments occurs between E and F, and between B and C.

The Scale always takes its name from the letter, or sound, on which it is based.

The *Key* is the governing sound: *it* governs the *pitch* of all the other sounds in the scale.

NOTE.—This and the succeeding scales should be practised until the pupils become perfectly familiar with all the sounds, syllables, and intervals, ascending and descending, in regular succession; then by skips, as 1—3—5—8; 1—5; 1—8, &c., until the pupils can give the sound of any note in the scale.

☞ In pronouncing Faw, Law, *a* should have the second sound, as in *far.*

G SCALE.

The notes on the staff represent musical sounds for both vocal and instrumental music.

The letters represent the sounds on the instrument, and the spaces between the letters represent the whole and half-intervals.

The numerals 1, 2, 3, &c., represent the sounds; and the spaces between the numerals represent the whole and half-intervals as produced by the voice.

In the Key of G, the voice and instrument ascend together to the sixth degree of the scale, when, as it will be seen at once, the intermediate sound from F to G must be played on the instrument, to conform to the natural rise of a whole interval from 6 to 7 in the voice.

A sound thus raised a half-interval on the instrument is said to be *sharped*,—marked thus, #, in the signature. Hence the Rule.—When G is the key, F must be played sharp to form the natural 7th of the Scale.

☞ A flat 7th in the Key of G is played on F, (on the instrument,) the note representing the flat 7th in a tune, will be marked with a natural, thus, ♮▽

D SCALE.

In this scale, the sound called D on the instrument, is taken as the key. The *natural* rise and fall of the voice from 1 to 2 is a whole-step, from 2 to 3 a whole-step, from 3 to 4 a half-step, from 4 to 5 a whole-step, from 5 to 6 a whole-step, from 6 to 7 a whole-step, and from 7 to 8 a half-step.

INSTRUMENTAL.—RULE.—When D is the key, F must be played sharp to form the natural 3rd of the scale; and C must be played sharp to form the natural 7th of the scale.

☞ A flat third in the key of D is played on F, on the instrument, and a flat seventh is played on C. These notes in the tunes will be marked thus, ♮▽, ♮▽.

A. SCALE.

KEY OF A.

Doe,	Ray,	Mee, Faw,	Sole,	Law,	See, Doe.	} *Voice.*
1	2	3 4	5	6	7 8	
A	B C#	D	E F#	G#	A	*Instrument.*

The 8th degree of this scale is *one*, or the key, to the next octave above.

The natural rise and fall of the voice is always the same, whatever may be the pitch of the key.

INSTRUMENTAL.—RULE.—When A is the key, F, C, and G must be played sharp to form the natural succession of intervals from the key,—or to make the instrument correspond with the natural rise and fall of the voice.

This scale of notes may be performed by assuming A flat as the key; then observe the following

RULE.—When A♭ is the key, B, E, A, and D must be played flat. The tune will have four flats in the signature, that is, at the first of the tune.

NOTE.—Instruments are constructed upon a chromatic scale; that is, a scale rising in half intervals from the lowest sound on the instrument to the highest. The sharp of one letter is the same sound as the flat of the next letter above it, so that G# is A♭; A# is B♭; C# is D♭; D# is E♭, and F# is G♭.

F SCALE.

KEY OF F.

Doe,	Ray,	Mee, Faw,	Sole,	Law,	See, Doe.	} *Voice.*
1	2	3 4	5	6	7 8	
Key—F	G	A ♭ B	C	D	E F	*Instrument.*

In this scale, F on the instrument is taken as the key. From F to G is a whole-interval,—from G to A is a whole-interval. From A to B is a whole-interval; but this will not correspond with the voice, which naturally rises and falls a half-interval between 3 and 4. We must therefore play the intermediate sound from A to B, called B flat,—marked thus, ♭, in the signature.

RULE.—When F is the key, B must be played flat on the instrument to form the natural 4th of the scale.

☞ A sharp 4th (#△) in the Key of F is played B natural on the instrument; and the note in the tune will be marked with a natural, thus, ♮△.

Bb SCALE.

KEY OF Bb

Doe, Ray, Mee, Faw, Sole, Law, See, Doe.} *Voice.*
1   2   3   4   5   6   7   8 Key

b B C D b E F G A b B *Inst.*

In this scale, the sound called B flat on the instrument is taken as the key.

The natural rise and fall of the voice is always the same, whatever may be the pitch of the key.

INSTRUMENTAL.—RULE.—When B flat is the key, B and E must be played flat to form the natural intervals in the scale from the key, or to make the instrument correspond with the natural rise and fall of the voice.

☞ Take B on the instrument as the key, and it will be necessary to play five sharps, in order to make the instrument correspond with the natural rise and fall of the voice.

Eb SCALE.

KEY OF Eb.

Doe, Ray, Mee, Faw, Sole, Law, See, Doe.} *Voice.*
1   2   3   4   5   6   7   8

Key—b E F G b A b B C D b E *Inst.*

In this scale, E flat on the instrument is taken as the key, it is, therefore, called the E flat scale.

The voice ascends and descends the octave by the same intervals in this scale as in all the preceding scales.

INSTRUMENTAL.—RULE.—When E flat is the key; B, E, and A, must be played flat. This scale of notes may be performed on the instrument by taking E as the key; then observe the following rule:—

When E is the key, F, C, G, and D must be played sharp.

☞ The notes *Doe, Ray, Mee,* &c., will occupy the same lines and spaces on the staff, and the natural rise and fall of the voice will be the same in the Key of E as in the Key of Eb.—The whole scale in Eb, is a half-interval lower than in E.

The preceding illustrations show the location of the scale on every letter on the staff, and it should be distinctly understood, that the Scale has a *permanent* location on each letter on the staff, and cannot be transposed.

We have now given a full explanation of all the sounds and intervals in one octave. If the voice is extended either above or below the octave, it will *naturally* pass over the same gradation, or succession of sounds and intervals, as far as the compass of the voice extends. Consequently, as the octaves are all alike, when one octave is understood all is understood in respect to pitch, or high and low sounds, in vocal music.

SECOND DEPARTMENT.—LENGTH OF SOUNDS.

THE consideration of the length of sounds naturally follows that of pitch. The first question in regard to notes is, What sounds do they represent? Or what is their pitch? The second question is, How long are these sounds to be continued?

We have heretofore considered sounds in reference only to their pitch, and their relation to each other as high or low.

The pitch of sounds is not affected by their length. The same sounds, of whatever pitch, may be continued for a longer or shorter time.

The notes (Doe, Ray, Mee, Faw, Sole, Law, See,) which represent *pitch*, also represent *length*, by adding a stem, filling the head of the note, &c., as follows:—

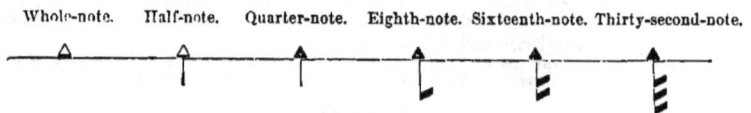

| Whole-note. | Half-note. | Quarter-note. | Eighth-note. | Sixteenth-note. | Thirty-second-note. |

These notes represent six varieties of length, each note having its appropriate name expressive of its relative length. On the half-note, the sound must be continued half as long as the whole-note; on the quarter-note, the sound must be continued quarter as long as the whole-note, &c., each note claiming its relative length in comparison with the others,—so that the whole-note represents the longest sound, and the thirty-second-note the shortest.

A *dot* (·) adds to a note one-half its length.

Thus, a dotted half-note ♩· is equal to three quarters ♩ ♩ ♩ or ♩ ♩

A dotted quarter ♪· is equal to three eighths ♫ ♫ ♫ or ♪ ♫

There are six different rests, or marks of silence, corresponding in time to the six different kinds of notes, as follows:—

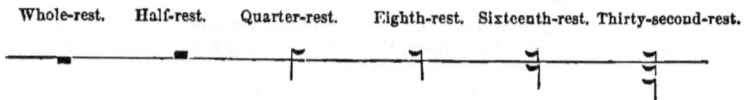

| Whole-rest. | Half-rest. | Quarter-rest. | Eighth-rest. | Sixteenth-rest. | Thirty-second-rest. |

A *dot* (·) adds to a rest one-half its length.

A *pause* (∧) is sometimes used. The notes over or under which it is written are to be prolonged indefinitely at the pleasure of the performer.

Staccato.—When a note, or several notes, are to be sung in a short, pointed, and distinct manner, the *staccato* (❜) is used. Dots (....) over or under the notes, signify *semi-staccato.*

Slur.—When one syllable of poetry is to be applied to two or more notes, a *slur* is drawn over or under the notes, or the stems of the notes are connected.

Triplet.—When three notes are to be sung in the time of two of the same value, the figure 3 is written over or under them.

Repeat.—A dotted line across the staff indicates a repetition.

A *Double bar* (|) shows the end of a strain of the music, or of a line of the poetry.

EXAMPLES.

| Pause. | Staccato. | Slur. | Stems connected. |

| Triplet. | Repeat. | Double bar. | Close of a tune. |

Measures.—Tunes are divided, by the single bar, into equal portions, called *measures.*

| Bar. | Bar. | Bar. | Bar. |

Each measure, or portion between the bars, must occupy the same time in the performance, (in the same tune) whatever may be the number of the notes in the measure.

To regulate the time, and to preserve an equal movement in the performance of a piece of music, certain regular motions of the hand are made; this is called *beating time,* or *keeping time.*

Two over two $\frac{2}{2}$ has two beats to the measure, the first *down,* the second *up,* with one half-note, or its value, to each beat in the measure, and is called *Double-time,* or *Two-two time.* Accented on the first part of the measure.

Three over two $\frac{3}{2}$ has three beats to the measure, the first *down,* the second *left,* the third *up,* with one half-note, or its value, to each beat in the measure, and is called *Triple-time,* or *Three-two time.* Accented on the first part of the measure.

Four over four $\frac{4}{4}$ has four beats to the measure, the first *down,* second *left,* (horizontally to the breast,) third *right,* (horizontally from the breast,) fourth *up,* with one quarter-note, or its value, to each beat in the measure, and is called *Quadruple time,* or *Four-four time.* Accented on the first and third parts of the measure.

Two over four $\frac{2}{4}$ has two beats to the measure, the first *down,* the second *up,* with one quarter-note, or its value, to each beat in the measure, and is called *Double-time,* or *Two-four time,* (second variety.) Accented on the first, part of the measure.

Three over four $\frac{3}{4}$ has three beats to the measure, the first beat *down,* second *left,* third *up,* with one quarter-note, or its value, to each beat in the measure, and is called *Triple-time,* or *Three-two time.* (second variety.)

Six over four $\frac{6}{4}$ has two beats to the measure, the first *down,* the second *up,* with a dotted half-note, or its value, to each beat in the measure, and is called *Compound-time,* or *Six-four time.* Accented on the first and fourth parts of the measure.

Nine over four $\frac{9}{4}$ has three beats to the measure, the first *down,* second *left,* third *up,* with three quarter notes, or their value, to each beat, and is called *Nine-four time,* or *Compound Triple-time.* Accented on the 1st, 4th, and 7th, parts of the measure.

RULE.—☞ The downward beat always begins the measure in all kinds of time.

Accent is a certain stress or force of voice upon what are termed the accented parts of the measure, and is as important in singing as in speaking. If the poetry be regular in its construction, and is properly adapted to the music, the accentuation of the two will correspond. If otherwise, that of the former must be attended to, and the musical accent be made to conform to the poetry.

PRACTICAL EXERCISES.

TWO-TWO TIME, OR DOUBLE-TIME.

THREE-TWO TIME, OR TRIPLE-TIME.

FOUR-FOUR TIME, OR QUADRUPLE-TIME.

TWO-FOUR TIME, OR DOUBLE-TIME.

THREE-FOUR TIME, OR TRIPLE-TIME.

SIX-FOUR TIME, OR COMPOUND-TIME.

NINE-FOUR TIME.

PRACTICAL EXERCISES.

STACCATO.

A *Slur* is used to show how many notes are to be sung to one syllable of the poetry. The slur is also used to denote the *legato* style.

LEGATO.—In a close, smooth, connected style.

His   beams   through   all   the   na - tions   run.

NOTES OF SYNCOPATION.

When an unaccented note is connected with the following accented note, it is said to be syncopated. Two notes tied together with a slur, represent one sound.

Doe   Ray   Mee...   Faw   Sole.....   Law   Sole.....   Faw   Mee.....   Ray Ray   Doe.

TRIPLETS.

THIRD DEPARTMENT.—Force of Sounds.

Musical sounds may be loud, very loud, soft, very soft, moderate, or ordinary as to force, without affecting their pitch or length.

Medium.—A sound produced by the ordinary action of the organs of voice, or of an instrument, is a *medium* sound, and is marked *m*.

Piano.—A sound produced by the vocal organs somewhat restrained, is a *soft* tone; it is called *piano*, and is marked *p*.

Pianissimo.—A sound produced by a very slight exertion of the vocal organs, yet so as to be distinctly audible, is called *pianissimo*, and is marked *pp*.

Forte —A loud sound, called *forte*, is produced by a strong and full exertion of the vocal organs. It is marked *f*.

Fortissimo.—A very loud sound is called *fortissimo;* it must not be attempted beyond the power of the vocal organs so as to degenerate into a scream. It is marked *ff*.

Accent.—General Rules. 1st. The first note in every measure must be accented.

2d. When there is more than one note to a beat, the first is accented.

3d. In triple-time, when the measure is filled with two quarter-notes, and two half-notes, the first half-note is accented.

In quadruple-time, the first and third parts of the measure are accented.

In compound-time, the first and fourth notes in the measure are accented.

Organ tone.—A sound which is commenced, continued, and ended with an equal degree of force or power, is called an organ tone (══════.)

Diminishing sound.—A sound commencing loud, and gradually diminished until it becomes soft, is marked *Dim.*, or ▷; also called *Diminuendo.*

Increasing sound.—A sound commencing soft and gradually increased until it becomes loud, is marked *Cres.*, or ◁; also called *Crescendo.*

Swell.—A sound commencing soft and gradually increased till it becomes loud, then diminished till it becomes soft, is marked thus ◁▷.

Pressure tone.—A very sudden swell is marked thus ◇.

Explosive tone.—When a sound is to be struck with great force, and instantly diminished, it is marked thus > or ◇.

PRACTICAL EXERCISE.

The Relative Value of the Six different kinds of Notes.

The Whole note is equal to

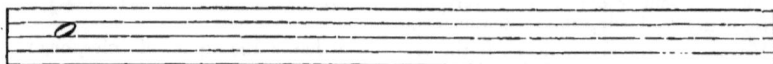

Two Halves,

Four Quarters,

Eight Eighths,

Sixteen Sixteenths, or

Thirty-two Thirty-seconds.

TIME LESSONS IN SCALE EXERCISES.

The following Ten lessons, in Scale Exercises, will be found to be the best that have ever been written for the rapid advancement of the Student in obtaining a practical knowledge of keeping Time. These lessons should be practised thoroughly, ascending and descending the octave; at the same time giving one beat (a motion of the right hand,) to the note claiming a beat, or its value, in all the different kinds of time. Then by skips, ♩, ♪, ♪, ♩, &c.

No. 1.

$\frac{2}{2}$ Time. Two beats to the measure. One beat to the half-note; two to the whole note; and two quarter-notes to the beat.

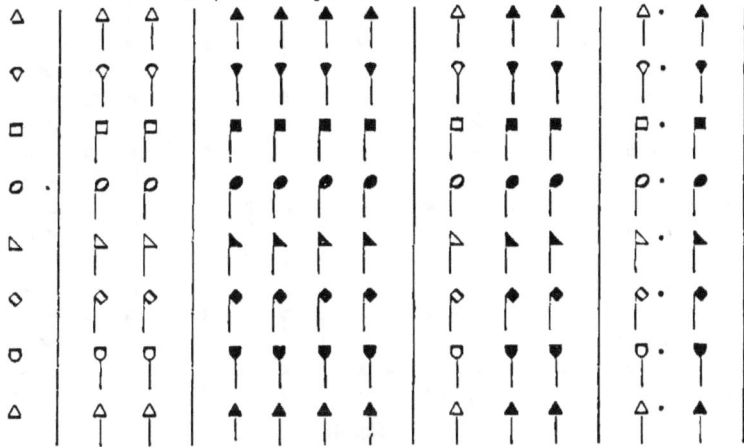

No. 2.

$\frac{2}{2}$ Time. Two beats to the measure.

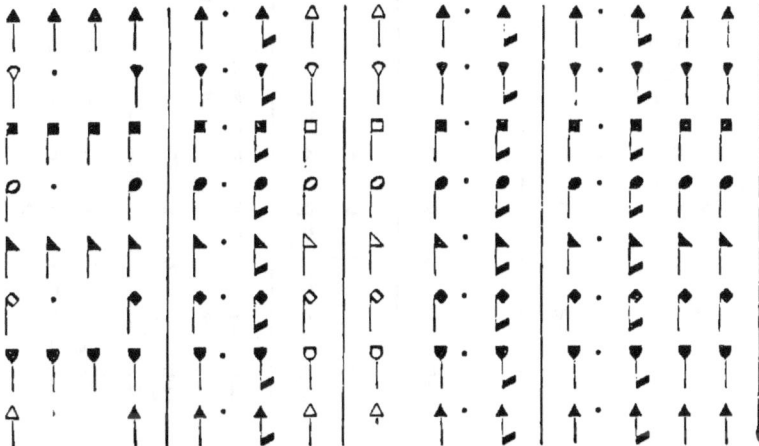

No. 3.

$\frac{2}{2}$ Time. Two beats to the measure.

No. 4.

$\frac{2}{2}$ Time. Two beats to the measure. A square block *on* the line is a Half rest. It has one beat in silence.

No. 5.

$\frac{3}{2}$ Time. Three beats to the measure. One beat to the half-note, or its value.

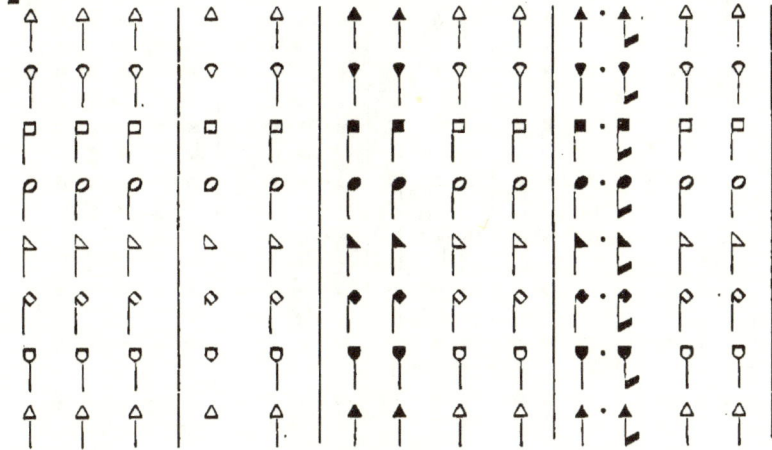

No. 6.

$\frac{3}{2}$ Time. Three beats to the measure. A square block *on* the line is a Half rest.
A square block *under* the line is a whole rest.

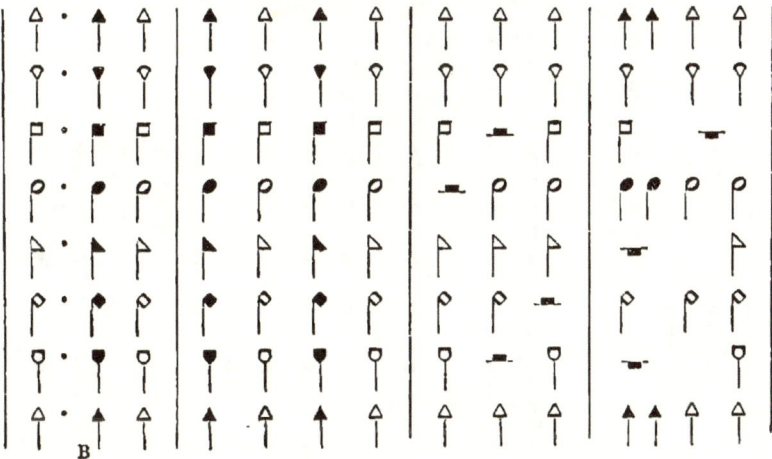

No. 7.

$\frac{4}{4}$ Time. Four beats to the measure. One beat to the Quarter note, or its value.

No. 8.

$\frac{4}{4}$ Time. Four beats to the measure.

No. 9.

$\frac{2}{4}$ Time. Two beats to the measure. One beat to the Quarter note, or its value.

No. 10.

$\frac{3}{4}$ Time. Three beats to the measure. One beat to the Quarter note, or its value.

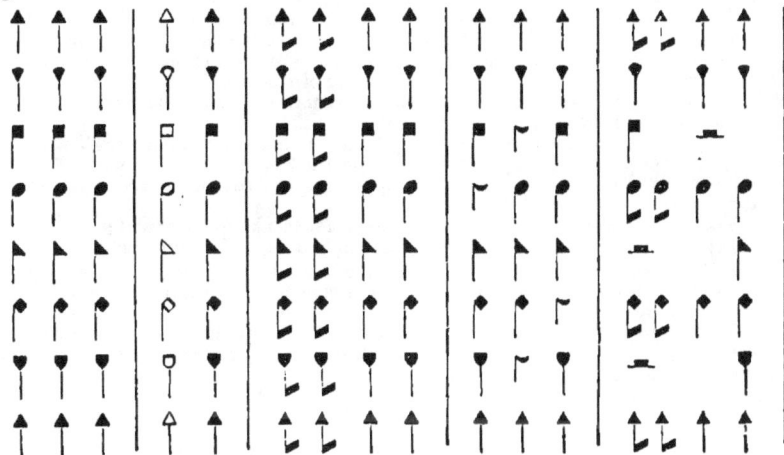

Doe	Dee	Ray	Ree	Mee	Faw	Fee	Sole	See	Law	Lee	See	Doe
1	♯1	2	♯2	3	4	♯4	5	♯5	6	♯6	7	8
C	♯C	D	♯D	E	F	♯F	G	♯G	A	♯A	B	C

Doe	See	Say	Law	Lay	Sole	Say	Faw	Mee	May	Ray	Raw	Doe
8	7	♭7	6	♭6	5	♭5	4	3	♭3	2	♭2	1
C	B	♭B	A	♭A	G	♭G	F	E	♭E	D	♭D	C

The singer, and performer on the instrument, should practise this scale together. It must be remembered that the *letters* are the *names* of the instrumental sounds, and represent sounds of *absolute pitch*, while the numerals and syllables represent the tones of the voice of *relative pitch*. It will be seen here that the notes representing intermediate sounds may be written on the same line or space of the staff with either of the notes between which they occur. Thus, the note representing the sound between 1 and 2 may be written on the same line or space with either of those notes. 1 may be elevated a half-interval, or 2 may be depressed a half-interval, and the same sound will be produced.

If it is proposed to elevate the lower sound, a ♯ is used, and the sound is called sharp 1, or (♯△,) sharp 4, or (♯△,) &c.

If it is prosposed to depress the upper sound, a ♭ (the sign of depression) is used, and the sound is called flat 3, or (♭○,) flat 7, or (♭♡,) &c.

There is also another character used in written music called the *Natural*, thus (♮,) which cancels or annuls the effect of either the sharp or the flat on the instrument.

When a natural occurs as an accidental, to restore sounds that have been *flatted in the signature*, it must be sung the same as in the case of a sharp.

When a natural occurs as an accidental, to restore sounds that have been *sharped in the signature*, it must be sung the same as that of a flat.

When sharp *one*, sharp *two*, sharp *four*, sharp *five*, sharp *six;* or flat *seven*, flat *six*, flat *five*, flat *three*, or flat *two* occur in a composition, (that is, in a tune,) the sharp ♯ or flat (♭) is prefixed to the note which the composer wishes sharp or flat, and in this respect they are termed *Accidental* flats and sharps.

The rule is, a sharp (♯) elevates the pitch of a note a half-step, or half-interval, and a flat (♭) depresses or lowers the pitch of a note a half-step, or half-interval.

☞ An accidental sharp (♯) or flat (♭) affects not only the one note before which it is placed, but also the following notes on the same letter or degree of the staff in the same measure.

When a natural occurs with a sharped note preceding it in the same measure, or a flatted note preceding it, the natural takes away the effect of the sharp or the flat, and the note must be sung or played natural.

Music is written upon two, three, or four staffs, joined together by a brace, thus:

This character ⎣ ⎦ is called the Treble, or G cleff, and shows the location of the seven letters on the lines and spaces of the Treble, Alto, and Tenor staffs.

This character ⎣ ⎦ is called the Base, or F cleff, and shows the location of the seven letters on the lines and spaces of the Base staff, as follows.

The following are the Signatures to the different Keys in common use.

KEY C.   KEY OF G.   KEY OF D.   KEY OF A.   KEY OF E.

KEY OF F.   KEY OF B♭.   KEY OF E♭.   KEY OF A♭

☞ One sharp (♯) is the key of G; two sharps, D; three sharps, A; four sharps, E. One (♭) is the key of F; two flats, B♭; three flats, E♭; four flats, A♭; no flats and sharps and the key is C.

PERFECT CHORDS OF THE SCALE.

First practise, and commit to memory, the chords of the scale. Play the three notes on the treble staff with the right hand (highest notes with the little finger) and the two notes on the base staff with the left hand, in octaves. After the chords of the scale are thoroughly committed to memory, commence with the plainest tunes in this book. Read only the treble notes, and play them with the chord notes on the treble and base staffs, as in the above scale. Continue to practise in this way until—keeping your eyes on the notes and not watching your fingers—you can play any plain tune in the book. When this is accomplished, commit to memory the following chords of the treble and base, and read and play the treble notes and base notes as they are written in the tunes.

FULL CHORDS ON THE TREBLE AND BASE.

Some of the Chords and Combinations which produce the Plaintive strains of music.

BANK OF KEYS FOR THE ORGAN,
WITH THE CORRESPONDING LETTERS ON THE STAFFS.

It will be seen by this representation of the Bank of Keys that every succession of eight sounds—as from C to C inclusively—is an octave; each octave is exactly the same in respect to the names of the keys. This may be rendered striking, even at first sight, by observing that C is always on the left of *two black keys;* and F is always on the left of *three black keys.*

The short, or black keys, serve for the sharps and flats. The black key between C and D is C♯ or D♭; the black key between D and E is D♯ or E♭; the black key between F and G is F♯ or G♭; the black key between G and A is G♯ or A♭; and the black key between A and B is A♯ or B♭. Thus the sharp of one *letter* is always the flat of the next *letter* above it.

23

BANK OF KEYS FOR THE ORGAN,

WITH THE CORRESPONDING NOTES ON THE STAFFS.

TREBLE.

BASE.

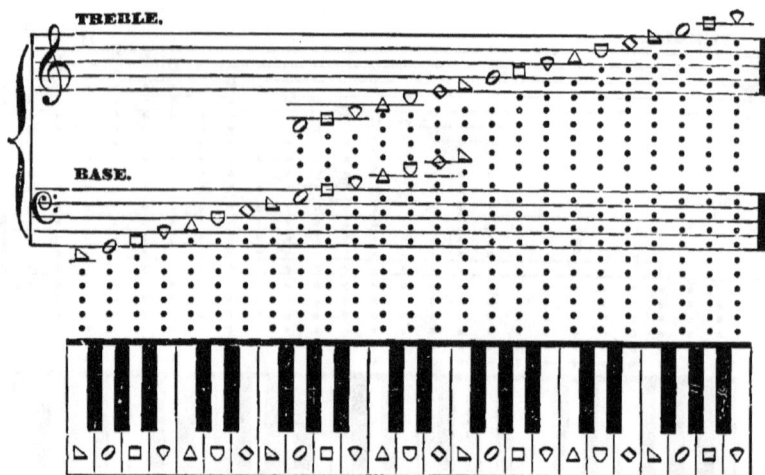

It will be seen by this representation of the Bank of Keys that every succession of eight sounds—as from △ to △ inclusively—is an octave; each octave is exactly the same in respect to the names of the keys. This may be rendered striking, even at first sight, by observing that △ is always on the left of *two black keys;* and ◩ is always on the left of *three black keys.* The short, or black keys, serve for the sharps and flats. The black key between △ and ○ is △♯ or ○♭; the black key between ○ and ◇ is ○♯ or ◇♭; the black key between ◩ and ○ is ◩♯ or ○♭; the black key between ○ and □ is ○♯ or □♭; and the black key between □ and ▽ is □♯ or ▽♭. Thus the sharp of one note is always the flat of the next note above it.

REMARKS.—In learning to play on the instrument by the syllables, (Doe, Ray, Mee, &c.) which the student can do by having an instrument with Transposing Bank of Keys, he will learn to sing and play at the same time. It must be remembered when a natural (♮) is prefixed to a note in a tune which has SHARPS for the signature, the note must be sung and played a half-interval lower—the same as when an accidental flat occurs in the same key, or same tune. And when a natural is prefixed to a note in a tune with FLATS for the signature, the note must be sung and played a half-interval higher—the same as when an accidental sharp occurs in the same tune.

When a natural occurs with a sharped note preceding it in the *same measure,* or a flatted note preceding it in the *same measure,* the natural takes away the effect of the sharp or flat, and the note must be sung and played *natural.*

In playing by the syllables, the Bank of Keys must be transposed into the key in which the tune is written, which can be done by means of the little knob in front of the Bank of Keys. Any tune can be played higher or lower than the key in which it is written, by transposing the Bank of Keys, instead of transposing the tune, while the notes may be played as they are written.

OLD HUNDRED. L. M.

Praise God, from whom all blessings flow, Praise him, all creatures here be-low;

Praise him a-bove, ye heavenly host, Praise Father, Son, and Ho-ly Ghost.

25

ROCKINGHAM. L. M.

1. Lord, I am thine, en - tire-ly thine, Purchased and saved by blood divine;

2. Here, Lord, my flesh, my soul, my all, I yield to thee be-yond re - call;

3. Grant one poor sin - ner more a place Among the children of thy grace;

4. Thee my new Mas - ter now I call, And con - se-crate to thee my all;
5. Do thou as - sist a fee - ble worm The great en-gage - ment to per-form:

With full con-sent thine I would be, And own thy sovereign right in me.

Ac-cept thy own, so long withheld; Ac-cept what I so free - ly yield.

A wretched sin - ner, lost to God, But ransom'd by Im-man-uel's blood.

Thine would I live, thine would I die, Be thine through all e - ter - ni - ty.
Thy grace can full as - sist-ance lend, And on that grace I dare de-pend.

UXBRIDGE. L. M.

Dr. L. MASON.

1. The heav'ns declare thy glory, Lord; In ev' - ry star thy wis - dom shines;

2. The rolling sun, the changing light, And nights and days, thy power confess;

3. Sun, moon, and stars convey thy praise Round the whole earth, and never stand;
4. Nor shall thy spreading gospel rest, Till through the world thy truth has run;

5. Great Sun of Righteousness, arise; Bless the dark world with heav'nly light;
6. Thy noblest wonders here we view, In souls renew'd, and sins for - giv'n;

But when our eyes be - hold thy word, We read thy name in fair - er lines.

But the blest volume thou hast writ Reveals thy justice and thy grace.

So when thy truth be-gan its race, It touch'd and glanced on ev'ry land.
Till Christ has all the nations bless'd, That see the light, or feel the sun.

Thy gos-pel makes the sim - ple wise, Thy laws are pure, thy judgments right.
Lord, cleanse my sins, my soul renew And make thy word my guide to heav'n.

HEBRON. L. M.

Dr. L. Mason.

1. As - sembled in our school once more, O Lord, thy bless-ing we implore;

2. Our fervent pray'r to thee ascends, For parents, teachers, foes, and friends;

3. When we on earth shall meet no more, May we a - bove to glo - ry soar,

We meet to read, and sing, and pray, Be with us, then, through this thy day.

And when we in thy house appear, Help us to worship in thy fear.

And praise thee in more lofty strains, Where one e - ter - nal Sabbath reigns.

L. O. EMERSON.

1. While life prolongs its precious light, Mercy is found and peace is giv'n;

2. While God invites, how blest the day! How sweet the gospel's charming sound!

3. Soon, borne on Time's most rapid wing, Shall death command you to the grave;

4. In that lone land of deep de - spair, No Sabbath's heav'nly light shall rise,

5. Now God in - vites; how blest the day! How sweet the gospel's charming sound!

But soon, ah, soon, approaching night Shall blot out ev' - ry hope of heav'n.

Come, sinners, haste, oh, haste away, While yet a pard' - ning God is found.

Be - fore his bar your spirits bring, And none be found to hear or save.

No God re-gard your bit-ter pray'r, No Saviour call you to the skies.

Come, sinners, haste, oh, haste away, While yet a pard' - ning God is found.

DUKE STREET. L. M.

1. Lord, when thou didst as-cend on high, Ten thousand angels fill'd the sky;

2. Not Sinai's mountain could appear More glorious, when the Lord was there;

3. Raised by his Fa-ther to the throne, He sent his promised Spirit down,

Those heav'nly guards around thee wait, Like chariots that at-tend thy state.

While he pronounced his dreadful law And struck the cho-sen tribes with awe.

With gifts and grace for reb-el men, That God might dwell on earth a-gain.

1. Oh, come, loud anthems let us sing, Loud thanks to our al-might-y King;

2. In - to his presence let us haste, To thank him for his fa - vours past;

3. Oh, let us to his courts repair, And bow with a - do - ra - tion there;

For we our voices high should raise, When our salvation's rock we praise.

To him address, in joy - ful song, Praises which to his name be-long.

Down on our knees, de-vout-ly, all Be-fore the Lord, our Maker, fall.

PETERBORO. C. M.

1. Once more, my soul, the ris - ing day   Sa - lutes my wak - ing eyes:

2. 'Tis he   supports   my mor - tal frame; My tongue shall speak his praise;

3. How ma - ny   wretched souls have fled Since the   last set - ting sun!

4. Great God, let   all   my hours be thine, While I   en - joy   the light;

Once more, my voice, thy tribute   pay   To Him   who rules the   skies.

My sins would rouse his wrath to flame, And   yet   his wrath de - lays.

And yet thou length'nest out my thread, And yet   my mo - ments run.

Then shall my sun in smiles de-cline, And   bring   a   peace-ful   night.

1. Let not de-spair nor fell re-venge Be to my bo - som known;

2. Feed me, O Lord, with need - ful food; I ask not wealth, nor fame;

3. Oh, may my days ob-scure - ly pass, Without re-morse or care,

Oh, give me tears for oth - ers' woes, And pa - tience for my own.

But give me eyes to view thy works, A heart to praise thy name.

And let me for my part - ing hour From day to day pre - pare.

MEAR. C. M.

Moderate.

1. Sing to the Lord, ye dis-tant lands, Ye tribes of ev'-ry tongue;

2. Say to the na-tions, Je-sus reigns, God's own al-migh-ty Son;

3. Let heav'n proclaim the joy-ful day, Joy through the earth be seen;

4. Let an un-u-sual joy sur-prise The isl-ands of the sea;
5. Be-hold, he comes, he comes to bless The na-tions, as their God,

His new-dis-cov-er'd grace de-mands A new and no-bler song.

His pow'r the sink-ing world sus-tains, And grace surrounds his throne.

Let ci-ties shine in bright ar-ray, And fields in cheer-ful green.

Ye mountains, sink, ye val-leys, rise, Pre-pare the Lord his way.
To show the world his right-eous-ness, And send his truth a-broad.

1. Oh, hap - py is the man who hears In - struc-tion's warn - ing voice;

2. For she has trea-sures great - er far Than east or west un - fold;

3. Her right hand of - fers to the just Im - mor - tal, hap - py days;

4. And as her ho - ly la - bours rise, So her re-wards in-crease;

And who ce - les - tial wis - dom makes His ear - ly, on - ly choice.

More pre-cious are her bright re-wards Than gems or stars of gold.

Her left, im - per - ish - a - ble wealth And heav'n-ly crowns dis - plays.

Her ways are ways of plea - sant - ness, And all her paths are peace.

EVAN. C. M.

Slowly. Gently.

1. In mer - cy, Lord, re-mem-ber me, Through all the hours of night,

2. With cheerful heart I close my eyes, Since thou wilt not re-move:

3. Or, if this night should prove the last, And end my tran-sient days,

And grant to me most gra - cious-ly The safe-guard of thy might.

Oh, in the morn-ing let me rise Re-joic-ing in thy love.

Oh, take me to thy promised rest, Where I may sing thy praise.

SCOTTISH.

1. O thou whose ten - der mer - cy hears Con - tri - tion's hum-ble sigh;

2. See, low be - fore the throne of grace, A wretch-ed wand'rer mourn;

3. And shall my guilt - y fears pre - vail To drive me from thy feet?

4. Oh, shine on this be - night - ed heart, With beams of mer - cy shine!

Whose hand, in - dul - gent, wipes the tears From sor - row's weep-ing eye:

Hast thou not bid me seek thy face? Hast thou not said, "Return"?

Oh, let not this dear ref - uge fail, This on - ly safe re - treat!

And let thy heal - ing voice im - part A taste of joys di - vine.

MARLOW. C. M.

1. Lord, I would own thy ten - der care, And all thy love to me;

2. And thou pre - serv - est me from death, And dan-gers ev' - ry hour:

3. My health, and friends, and pa - rents dear, To me by God are giv'n;

4. Such good-ness, Lord, and con - stant care, A child can ne'er re - pay;

The food I eat, the clothes I wear, Are all be - stow'd by thee.

I can - not draw an - oth - er breath, Un - less thou give the power.

I have not a - ny bless - ings here But what are sent from heav'n.

But may it be my dai - ly pray'r To love thee and o - bey.

SWAN.

1. Why do we mourn de-part-ing friends, Or shake at death's a-larms?

2. Are we not tend-ing up-ward, too, As fast as time can move?

3. Why should we trem-ble to con-vey Their bo-dies to the tomb?

4. The graves of all the saints he bless'd, And soft-en'd ev'-ry bed:
5. Thence he a-rose, as-cend-ed high, And show'd our feet the way:

'Tis but the voice that Je-sus sends To call them to his arms.

Nor should we wish the hours more slow To keep us from our love.

There the dear flesh of Je-sus lay, And left a sweet per-fume.

Where should the dy-ing mem-bers rest But with their dy-ing Head?
Up to the Lord our flesh shall fly, At the great ris-ing day.

ORTONVILLE. C. M.

1. Lord, teach a lit - tle child to pray; Thy grace betimes im-part; And grant thy

2. A fall-en creature I was born, And from my birth I stray'd: I must be

3. But Christ can all my sins for-give, And wash away their stain; Can fit my

4. To him let lit - tle children come, For he hath said they may; His bosom
5. For all who ear - ly seek his face Shall sure-ly taste his love; Je - sus shall

Ho - ly Spi - rit may Re - new my sin - ful heart, Re-new my sin - ful heart.

wretched and 'or-lorn With-out thy mer-cy's aid, Without thy mer-cy's aid.

soul with him to live, And in his kingdom reign, And in his kingdom reign.

then shall be their home, Their tears he'll wipe a-way, Their tears he'll wipe away.
guide them by his grace To dwell with him a-bove, To dwell with him a - bove.

OLIVER HOLDEN.

1. All hail the pow'r of Jesus' name! Let angels prostrate fall; Bring forth the royal di - a - dem,

2. Ye chosen seed of Israel's race, Ye ransom'd from the fall, Hail him who saves you by his grace,

3. Ye gentile sinners, ne'er forget The wormwood and the gall; Go, spread your trophies at his feet,

4. Let ev'-ry kindred, ev'-ry tribe, On this terrestrial ball, To him all ma-jes - ty as - cribe,
5. Oh that with yonder sacred throng We at his feet may fall; We'll join the ev-er-last - ing song,

And crown him Lord of all, Bring forth the royal di-a - dem, And crown him Lord   of all.

And crown him Lord of all, Hail him who saves you by his grace, And crown him Lord of all.

Aud crown him Lord of all, Go, spread your trophies at his feet, And crown him Lord of all.

And crown him Lord of all, To him all ma-jes-ty   ascribe, And crown him Lord   of all.
And crown him Lord of all! We'll join the everlasting song, And crown him Lord   of all!

FARNHAM. C. M. Double.

1. Soon as I heard my Father say, "Ye children, seek my grace," } Let not thy face be hid from me,
My heart replied, without delay, "I'll seek my Father's face." }

2. Should friends and kindred near and dear, Leave me to want or die,} Wait on the Lord, ye trembling saints,
My God will make my life his care, And all my need supply.}

Nor frown my soul a - way; God of my life, I fly to thee In each distress - ing day.

And keep your courage up; He'll raise your spi - rit when it faints, And far ex-ceed your hope.

1. My God, the spring of all my joys, The life of my de - lights,
The glo - ry of my bright-est days, And comfort of my nights,
D.C. Thou art my soul's bright morning star, And thou my ris - ing sun.

3. The op'n-ing heav'ns a-round me shine With beams of sa-cred bliss,
If Je - sus show his mer - cy mine, And whisper I am his.
Run up with joy the shining way, To see and praise my Lord.

2. In dark-est shades, if thou ap - pear, My dawning is be - gun;

4. My soul would leave this hea - vy clay At that transport-ing word,

ST. THOMAS. S. M.

A. WILLIAMS.

1. The Lord, the sov' - reign King, Has fix'd his throne on high,

2. Ye an - gels, great in might, And swift to do his will,

3. Ye heav'n-ly hosts, who wait The or - ders of your King,

4. While all his won - drous works, Through his vast king-dom, show

O'er all the heav'n-ly world he rules, And all be - neath the sky.

Bless ye the Lord, whose voice ye hear, Whose pleasure ye ful - fil.

Who guard his churches when they pray, Oh, join the praise we sing!

Their Ma - ker's glo - ry, thou, my soul, Shalt sing his gra - ces too.

Altered from D. READ.

1. Welcome, sweet day of rest, That saw the Lord a - rise,

2. Je - sus him - self comes near And feasts his saints to - day;

3. One day a - mid the place Where God my Sa - viour's been

4. My will - ing soul would stay In such a frame as this,

Welcome to this re - viv - ing breast And these re - joic - ing eyes.

Here we may sit and see him here, And love, and praise, and pray.

Is sweet - er than ten thousand days Of plea-sure and of sin.

Till call'd to rise and soar a - way To ev - er - last - ing bliss.

BOYLSTON. S. M.

Dr. L. Mason.

1. The pi - ty of the Lord, To those that fear his name,

2. He knows we are but dust, Scat - ter'd with ev' - ry breath;

3. Our days are as the grass, Or like the morn - ing flow'r;

4. But thy com - pas - sions, Lord, To end - less years en - dure;

Is such as ten - der pa - rents feel; He knows our fee - ble frame.

His an - ger, like a ris - ing wind, Can send us swift to death.

If one sharp blast sweep o'er the field, It with - ers in an hour.

And chil-dren's chil - dren ev - er find Thy words of prom - ise sure.

WESTERN TUNE.

1. With hum - ble heart and tongue, My God, to thee I pray:

2. Make an un - guard - ed youth The ob - ject of thy care;

3. My heart, to fol - ly prone, Re - new by pow'r di - vine;

4. Oh, let thy word of grace My warm - est thoughts em-ploy;

Oh, bring me now, while I am young, To thee, the liv - ing way.

Help me to choose the way of truth And fly from ev' - ry snare.

U - nite it to thy-self a - lone, And make me whol - ly thine.

Be this, through all my fol-lowing days, My trea - sure and my joy.

SHAWMUT. S. M.

1. Our heav'n - ly Fa - ther, hear   The   pray'r we of - fer now:

2. Thy   king - dom come; thy will   On   earth   be done   in   love.

3. Our   dai - ly bread sup - ply, While   by   thy word we   live;
4. From dark   temp-ta - tion's pow'r, From   Sa - tan's wiles de - fend;

5. Thine, then,   for - ev - er   be   Glo - ry   and pow'r di - vine;
6. Thus hum - bly taught to   pray   By   thy   be - lov - ed   Son,

Thy   name be hal-low'd far   and   near,   To   thee   all na - tions bow.

As   saints and ser - a - phim   ful - fil   Thy   per - fect law   a - bove.

The   guilt of our   in - i - qui - ty   For - give   as we   for - give.
De - liv - er   in   the e - vil hour, And   guide us   to   the end.

The   scep - tre, throne, and ma - jes - ty   Of   heav'n and earth are thine.
Through him we come to thee, and say, All   for   his sake   be done.

1. My God, my life, my love, To thee, to thee I call;

2. Thy shin-ing grace can cheer This dun-geon where I dwell;

3. To thee, and thee a-lone, The an-gels owe their bliss;

4. Not all the harps a-bove Can make a heav'n-ly place,
5. Nor earth, nor all the sky, Can one de-light af-ford,

I can-not live if thou re-move, For thou art all in all.

'Tis par-a-dise when thou art here, When thou de-part, 'tis hell.

They sit a-round thy gra-cious throne, And dwell where Je-sus is.

If God his res-i-dence re-move, Or but con-ceal his face.
D No, not a drop of re-al joy, With-out thy pre-sence, Lord.

1. O God, my in - most soul con - vert, And deep - ly on my thoughtful heart E-

2. Be - fore me place in dread ar - ray The pomp of that tre - men - dous day When

3. Be this my one great business here, With se - rious in - dus - try and fear E-

ternal things impress; { Cause me to feel their solemn weight, } And wake to righteousness.
                       { And trem-ble on the brink of fate, }

thou with clouds shalt come { To judge the nations at thy bar: } To meet a joy - ful doom.
                            { And tell me, Lord, shall I be there }

ternal bliss t' in-sure, { Thine utmost counsel to ful - fil, } And to the end en-dure.
                         { And suf - fer all thy righteous will, }

A. WILLIAMS.

1. The Lord Jehovah reigns, And royal state maintains; His head with awful glories crown'd;

2. Upheld by thy commands, The world securely stands, And skies and stars obey thy word;

3. In vain the noisy crowd, Like billows fierce and loud, Against thine empire rage and roar;

4. Let floods and nations rage, And all their pow'rs engage; Let swelling tides assault the sky:

Array'd in robes of light, Begirt with sov'reign might, And rays of majes - ty a - round.

Thy throne was fix'd on high Be - fore the starry sky: E - ter-nal is thy kingdom, Lord.

In vain with an-gry spite The sur- ly nations fight, And dash like waves against the shore.

The terrors of thy frown Shall beat their madness down: Thy throne forever stands on high.

1. Ye boundless realms of joy, Ex - alt your Ma - ker's name:
His praise your songs em - ploy: A - bove the star - ry frame

2. Let all a - dore the Lord, And praise his ho - ly name,
By whose al - migh - ty word They all from no - thing came;

Your voi-ces raise, Ye cher-u-bim And ser - a-phim, To sing his praise.

And all shall last, From changes free: His firm decree Stands ev - er fast.

Ritard.

Ritard.

Or 6 lines, by repeating the first two strains of the music.　　　From Rev. DR. MALAN.

1. To thy pastures, fair and large, Heav'nly Shepherd, lead thy charge; And my couch with

2. When I faint with summer's heat, Thou shalt guide my weary feet To the streams that,

3. Constant, to my lat - est end, Thou my foot-steps shalt at - tend, And shalt bid thy

4. Safe the drea - ry vale I tread, By the shades of death o'erspread: With thy rod and

tend'rest care Midst the springing grass pre - pare, Midst the springing grass pre - pare.

still and slow, Through the verdant meadows flow, Through the verdant meadows flow.

hallow'd dome Yield me an e - ter - nal home, Yield me an e - ter - nal home.

staff sup - plied, This my guard, and that my guide, This my guard, and that my guide.

ELTHAM. 7s. Double.

1. Hasten, Lord, the glorious time, When, beneath Mes-si - ah's sway, }
Ev' - ry na - tion, ev' - ry clime, Shall the gos - pel call o - bey. }
Sa - tan and his hosts o'erthrown, Bound in chains, shall hurt no more.

3. Then shall wars and tumults cease, Then be banish'd grief and pain; }
Righteousness, and jo .r peace, Un-disturb'd shall ev - er reign. }
All his migh - ty a c . - cord, All his wondrous love pro - claim.

2. Mightiest kings his pow'r shall own, Heathen tribes his name a - dore;

4. Bless we, then, our gracious Lord, Ev - er praise his glorious name;

1. Wake the song of ju - bi - lee, Let it e - cho o'er the sea!
Now is come the promised hour, Je - sus reigns with sov'reign pow'r!
Let it sound from shore to shore, Je - sus reigns for ev - er - more!

3. Now the de - sert lands re - joice, And the islands join their voice;
Yea, the whole cre - a - tion sings, "Je - sus is the King of kings!"
Let it sound from shore to shore, Je - sus reigns for ev - er - more!

2. All ye na - tions join and sing, "Christ of lords and kings is King!"

4. Wake the song of ju - bi - lee, Let it e - cho o'er the sea!

MARTYN. 7s. Double.

S. B. MARSH.

1. Ma - ry to the Saviour's tomb Hasted at the ear - ly· dawn; }
Spice she brought, and sweet perfume, But the Lord she loved had gone; }
Trembling, while the crystal flood Issued from her weep - ing eyes.

2. But her sor-rows quick-ly fled When she heard his welcome voice; }
Christ had risen from the dead, Now he bids her heart re - joice; }
Ye who weep for Je - sus' sake, He will wipe your tears a - way.

D.C.

For a-while she ling'ring stood, Fill'd with sorrow and sur - prise,

D.C.

What a change his word can make, Turning darkness in - to day!

1. Brethren, while we sojourn here, Fight we must, but should not fear; } { Forward, then, with
Foes we have, but we've a Friend, One that loves us to the end. } { Long we shall not

2. In the way a thousand snares Lie to take us un - a - wares; } { But, from Satan's
Sa - tan, with ma - li - cious art, Watch-es each un - guard - ed part: } { Saints shall soon vic-

3. But of all the foes we meet, None so oft mis - lead our feet, } { Yet let nothing
None betray us in - to sin, Like the foes that dwell with - in; } { Christ shall al - so

cour - age go, } Soon the joy - ful news will come, "Child, your Father calls, come home!"
dwell be - low; }

mal - ice free, }
to - rious be; }

spoil our peace, } Soon the joy - ful news will come, "Child, your Father calls, come home!"
con - quer these; }

58   **WEBB** 7s & 6s.

G. J. WEBB.

1st.   2d.

1. { The morn-ing light is break-ing, The dark-ness dis-ap-pears; } The sons of earth are wak-ing To pen-i................ten-tial tears; }
D.C. Of na-tions in com-mo-tion, Pre-par'd for................ Zi-on's war.

Fine.

2. { Rich dews of grace come o'er us, In many a gen-tle shower, } And bright-er scenes be-fore us Are op'n-ing................ ev'-ry hour; }
D.C. And heav'nly gales are blow-ing, With peace up-................on their wings.

Each breeze that sweeps the o-cean Brings tid-ings from a-far,

D.C.

Each cry to hea-ven go-ing, A-bun-dant an-swers bring.

D.C.

D.C.

3 See heathen nations oending
  Before the God we love,
And thousand hearts ascending
  In gratitude above;
While sinners, now confessing,
  The gospel call obey,
And seek the Saviour's blessing,
  A nation in a day.

4 Blest river of salvation,
  Pursue thy onward way;
Flow thou to ev'ry nation,
  Nor in thy richness stay:
Stay not till all the lowly
  Triumphant reach their home;
Stay not till all the holy
  Proclaim, The Lord is come.

PASS ME NOT.

W. H. DOANE.

1st.   **2d.**

1. { Pass me not, O gen- tle   Sa-viour, Hear my humble cry;
   { While on others thou art   call - ing,... Do not pass me   by. }

2. { Let me, at   a throne of   mer- cy, Find a sweet re - lief;
   { Kneeling there in deep contri-tion,...................................... Help my un-be - lief.

Chorus.

Saviour, Saviour, hear my humble cry,   While on others thou art calling, Do not pass me by.

Saviour, Saviour, hear my humble cry,   While on others thou art calling, Do not pass me by.

3 Trusting only in thy merit,
  Would I seek thy face;
  Heal my wounded, broken spirit,
  Save me by thy grace.
    Saviour, Saviour, &c.

4 Thou the spring of all my comfort,
  More than life to me;
  Whom have I on earth beside thee;
  Whom in heav'n but thee!
    Saviour, Saviour, &c.

CHESTER. 8s & 7s.

1. Je-sus! hear a weep-ing mourner, Hear a sin-ner poor and vile;

2. Friend of sinners! I have scorn'd thee, Scorn'd thy name, and scorn'd thy laws;

3. Plead my cause, with pow'r prevail-ing, At the sov'reign bar of God;

4. Lord of pi-ty! see me lan-guish At thy feet, and bid me live:

Hear me, once a wick-ed scorn-er, Now im-plore thy pi-tying smile.

Yet in mer-cy thou hast warn'd me, Yet in mer-cy plead my cause.

Save me from e-ter-nal wail-ing, Save me from Je-ho-vah's rod.

Thou a-lone canst ease my an-guish, Thou a-lone canst par-don give.

Slow movement.

1. Nearer, my God, to thee, Nearer to thee: E'en though it be a cross That raiseth me,

2. Tho' like a wanderer, Daylight all gone, Darkness be o-ver me, My rest a stone,

3. There let the way appear Steps up to heav'n; All that thou sendest me In mercy giv'n;

4. Then, with my waking thoughts Bright with thy praise, Out of my stony griefs Bethel I'll raise;
5. Or if, on joy-ful wing Cleaving the sky, Sun, moon, and stars forgot, Upward I fly,

Still all my song shall be, Nearer, my God, to thee, Nearer, my God, to thee, Nearer to thee.

Yet in my dreams I'd be Nearer, my God, to thee, Nearer, my God, to thee, Nearer to thee.

Angels to beckon me Nearer, my God, to thee, Nearer, my God, to thee, Nearer to thee.

So by my woes to be Nearer, my God, to thee, Nearer, my God, to thee, Nearer to thee.
Still all my song shall be, Nearer, my God, to thee, Nearer, my God, to thee, Nearer to thee.

SWEET HOUR OF PRAYER.

W. B. BRADBURY.

Slow, steady time.

1. Sweet hour of prayer! sweet hour of prayer! That calls me from a world of care,

2. Sweet hour of prayer! sweet hour of prayer! Thy wings shall my pe- ti - tion bear

3. Sweet hour of prayer! sweet hour of prayer! May I thy con - so - la -tion share;

And bids me at my Father's throne Make all my wants and wishes known:

To him whose truth and faith -ful -ness, En-gage the waiting soul to bless;

Till from Mount Pisgah's lof - ty height, I view my home, and take my flight;

In sea - sons of dis-tress and grief My soul has oft - en found re - lief;

And since he bids me seek his face, Be-lieve his word and trust his grace,

This robe of flesh I'll drop, and rise To seize the ev - er - last-ing prize;

And oft escaped the tempter's snare By thy re-turn, sweet hour of prayer.

I'll cast on him my ev' - ry care, And wait for him, sweet hour of prayer.

And shout, while passing through the air, Farewell, farewell, sweet hour of prayer.

SUNDAY-SCHOOL VOLUNTEER SONG.

WM. B. BRADBURY.

Marching movement.

1. We are marching on, with shield and banner bright, We will work for God, and battle for the right,
   In the Sunday-school our arm - y we prepare, As we rally round our blessed standard there,
   D.C. We are marching onward, singing as we go, To the promised land where living waters flow ;

2. We are marching on, our Cap-tain, ev - er near, Will protect us still, his gentle voice we hear ;
   Then awake, awake, our happy, happy song, We will shout for joy, and gladly march along:

3. We are marching on the straight and narrow way That will lead to life and everlasting day ;
   We are marching on, and pressing t'ward the prize, To a glorious crown beyond the glowing skies,

End.

We will praise his name, re - joic - ing in his might, And we'll work till Je - sus calls.
And the Saviour's cross we ear - ly learn to bear, While we work till Je - sus calls.
Come and join our ranks as pilgrims here be-low, Come and work till Je - sus calls.

Let the foe advance, we'll nev - er, nev - er fear, For we'll work till Je - sus calls.
In the Lord of Hosts let ev' - ry heart be strong, While we work till Je - sus calls.

End.

To the smil - ing fields that nev - er will de - cay, But we'll work till Je - sus calls.
To the ra - diant fields where pleasure nev - er dies, And we'll work till Je - sus calls.

Chorus.
Then awake, then awake, hap - py song,
Then a - wake, then a - wake, hap - py song, hap - py song, Shout for
Then awake, then awake, hap - py song, hap - py song,
D.C.
Shout for joy, shout for joy, As we glad - ly march a - long.
joy, shout for joy, As we glad - ly march a - long.
D.C.
Shout for joy, shout for joy, As we glad - ly march a - long.

THE VALLEY OF BLESSING.

Words by ANNIE WITTEMEYER.   W. G. FISCHER.

1. I have entered the valley of blessing so sweet, And Je-sus abides with me there;

2. There is peace in the valley of blessing so sweet, And plen-ty the land doth impart;

3. There is love in the valley of blessing so sweet, Such as none but the blood-wash'd may feel;
4. There's a song in the valley of blessing so sweet, That angels would fain join the strain—

And his Spirit and blood make my cleansing complete, And his perfect love casteth out fear.

There is rest for the weary-worn taveller's feet, And joy for the sor-row-ing heart.

When heav'n comes down redeemed spirits to greet, And Christ sets his covenant seal.
As, with rapturous praises, we bow at his feet, Crying, "Worthy the Lamb that was slain."

Oh, come to this val - ley of blessing so sweet, Where Jesus will fulness be - stow;

Oh, come to this val - ley of blessing so sweet, Where Jesus will fulness be - stow;

Oh, be-lieve, and receive, and con-fess him, That all his sal - va - tion may know.

Oh, be-lieve, and receive, and con-fess him, That all his sal - va - tion may know.

HARWELL. 8s & 7s. 6 lines. Peculiar.

1. Hark, ten thousand harps and voices Sound the note of praise above: }
Jesus reigns, and heav'n rejoices, Jesus reigns the God of love : } See he sits   on yonder

2. Jesus, hail! whose glory brightens All above, and gives it worth : }
Lord of life, thy smile enlightens, Cheers and charms thy saints on earth : } When we think of love like

3. King of glo-ry, reign for-ev - er, Thine an ev-er-last-ing crown ; }
Nothing from thy love shall sever Those whom thou hast made thine own : } Happy ob - jects of thy

throne, Jesus rules   the world alone. Hal-le - lu-jah! hal-le - lu-jah! hal-le - lu-jah! A - men.

thine,   Lord, we own it love di-vine. Hal-le - lu-jah! hal-le - lu-jah! hal-le - lu-jah! A - men.

grace, Destined to   behold thy face. Hal-le - lu-jah! hal-le - lu-jah! hal-le - lu-jah! A - men.

1. The Sun-day-school, that bless-ed place, Oh! I would ra-ther stay
Chorus. The Sun-day-school, the Sun-day-school, Oh! 'tis the place I love,

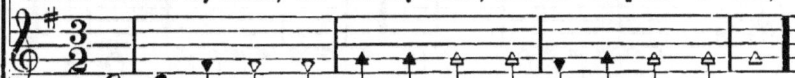

2. 'Tis there I learn that Je-sus died For sin-ners such as I;

3. Then let our grate-ful tri-bute rise, And songs of praise be given
Chorus. The Sun-day-school, the Sun-day-school, Oh! 'tis the place I love,

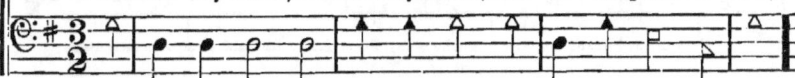

4. And welcome, then, the Sunday-school, We'll read, and sing, and pray,

With-in its walls, a child of grace, Than spend my hours in play.
For there I learn the gold-en rule, Which leads to joys a-bove.

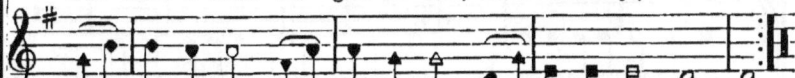

Oh! what has all the world be-side, That I should prize so high?

To Him who dwells a-bove the skies, For such a bless-ing given.
For there I learn the gold-en rule, Which leads to joys a-bove.

That we may keep the gold-en rule, And nev-er from it stray.

SAVANNAH. 10s.

PLEYEL.

1. Rise, crown'd with light, imperial Salem rise; Ex - alt thy tow'ring head, and lift thine eyes;

2. So a long race thy spacious courts adorn; See future sons and daughters yet un - born,

3. See barb'rous nations at thy gates attend, Walk in the light, and in thy tem - ple bend;

4. The seas shall waste, the skies to smoke decay, Rocks fall to dust, and mountains melt a-way;

See heav'n its sparkling portals wide display, And break up - on thee in a flood of day.

In crowding ranks on ev' - ry side a - rise, De - mand-ing life, im - patient for the skies.

See thy bright altars throng'd with prostrate kings, While ev'ry land its joyous tribute brings.

But, fix'd his word, his saving pow'r remains; Thy realm shall last, thy own Mes - si - ah reigns.

STAY, SINNER. L. M.

Words by Rev. W. Kenney.   Music by W. J. Kirkpatrick.

1. Stay, sin-ner, stay! the night comes on, When slighted mer - cy is withdrawn,
2. Stay, sin-ner, stay! the Fa-ther's call Now bids you come, for - sak-ing all:

3. Stay, sin-ner, stay! 'tis Je-sus pleads: For you he weeps, for you he bleeds;
4. Stay, sin-ner, stay! the Spi-rit cries, A-wake, and from the dead a-rise;

5. Stay, sin-ner, stay! your life, soon past, Will end in mourn-ing at the last,
6. Come, sin-ner, come! though guil-ty now, At Je-sus' feet sub-mis-sive bow,

7. Come, sin-ner, come! a home a-bove, Where all is light and joy and love,
8. See, sin-ner, see where loved ones stand, All saved in heav'n,—a hap-py land:

The Ho-ly Spi - rit strives no more, And Je-sus gives his plead-ings o'er.
Oh, come, and he will bid you live: Oh, come, and free - ly he'll for - give.

Oh, let his love your heart con-strain, Nor let him weep and bleed in vain.
A-rise, and plead for mer - cy now, And at the cross re-pent - ing bow.

As death's dark vale comes full in view, With none to guide you safe - ly through.
And free-ly all shall be for-giv'n: Oh, come, and taste the joys of heav'n.

In-vites you now to haste a - way To realms of ev - er - last - ing day.
Oh, come, and join them on that shore, Where death and part-ing are no more.

CLIMBING UP ZION'S HILL.

Words by Rev. J. G. Chapee.

Philip Phillips.

1. "I'm trying to climb up Zion's hill," For the Saviour whispers, "Love me;" Tho' all beneath is

Air.

2. I know I'm but a little child, My strength will not protect me; But then I am the

3. Then come with me, we'll upward go, And climb this hill to - geth-er; And as we walk, we'll

dark as death, Yet the stars are bright above me. Then upward still, To Zion's hill, To the land of joy and

Saviour's Lamb, And he will not neglect me. Then all the time I'll try to climb This ho - ly hill of

sweetly talk, And sing as we go thither. Then mount up still God's holy hill, Till we reach the pearly beauty, My path before Shines more and more, As it nears the gold - en ci - ty. I'm

Zi - on; For I am sure The way is pure, And on it comes "no li - on."

portals, Where raptured tongues Proclaim the songs Of the shining-robed im - mor - tals.

Climbing, climbing, climbing up Zion's hill.

I'm climbing up Zion's hill, Climbing, climbing, climbing up Zion's hill.

climbing up Zion's hill I'm climbing up Zion's hill, Climbing, climbing, climbing up Zion's hill.

Climbing, climbing, climbing up Zion's hill.

THE GOOD OLD WAY.

W. H. Doane.

1. We are going forth with our staff in hand, Thro' a desert wild in a stranger land;

2. There are foes without, there are foes within, They would turn us back to the paths of sin;

3. In the blissful hour of communion sweet, Let us come with joy to the Mercy seat;
4. On the brink of time when we stand at last, When our sun has set, and our work is past,

But our faith is bright, and our hope is strong, And the Good Old Way is our pilgrim song.

We will stop our ears to the words they say, While we onward press in the Good Old Way.

O, we love to sing, and we love to pray, And we bless the Lord for the Good Old Way.
When we bid farewell to our mortal clay, We will praise the Lord for the Good Old Way.

Chorus.

'Tis the Good Old Way, by our fathers trod, 'Tis the way of life, and it leadeth unto God:

'Tis the Good Old Way, by our fathers trod; 'Tis the way of life, and it leadeth unto God;

'Tis the only path to the realms of day; We are going home in the Good Old Way.

'Tis the only path to the realms of day; We are going home in the Good Old Way.

THE LAND OF BEULAH. C. M.

Words by Rev. J. HASKELL.

1. My lat - est sun is sink-ing fast, My race is near-ly run; My strongest tri - als

2. I know I'm near the ho - ly ranks Of friends and kindred dear; I brush the dews on

3. I've almost gain'd my heavenly home; My spir - it loud-ly sings; The ho - ly ones, be-

4. O, bear my longing heart to Him Who bled and died for me; Whose blood now cleanses

Chorus.

now are past, My tri - umph is be - gun. O come, an - gel band, Come, and a-

Jordan's banks, The cross-ing must be near. O come, an - gel band, Come, and a-

hold they come! I hear the noise of wings. O come, an - gel band, Come, and a-

from all sin, And gives me vic - to - ry. O come, &c.,

round me stand; O   bear me a - way on your snow-y wings To my im-mor-tal home, O

round me stand; O   bear me a - way on   your snow-y wings To my im-mor-tal   home, O

round me stand; O   bear me   a - way on   your snow-y wings To my im-mor - tal home, O

bear me   a - way   on   your snow - y   wings To my   im - mor - tal   home.

bear me   a - way   on   your snow - y   wings To my   im - mor - tal   home.

bear me   a - way   on   your snow - y   wings To my   im - mor - tal   home.

"GLORY, GLORY TO THE LAMB."

1. Hark! the sweetest notes of angels, singing, Glo-ry, glo-ry to the Lamb,

2. Ye for whom his precious life was giv-en, Sacred themes to you be - long;

3. Hearts all fill'd with ho-ly em - u - la - tion, We u - nite with those a - bove;

4. Endless life in Christ our Lord possessing, Let us praise his precious name;

All the hosts of heav'n their tribute bringing, Raising high the Saviour's name.

Come, and join the glorious choir of heaven, Join the ev - er-last - ing song.

Sweet the theme—the theme of free salvation, Founts of ev - er-last-ing love.

Glory, honor, riches, power, and blessing, Be for - ev - er to the Lamb.

Chorus.

We will join the beautiful an - gels, We will join the beautiful an - gels,

We will join the beautiful an - gels, We will join the beautiful an - gels,

We will join the beautiful an - gels, We will join the beautiful an - gels,

Sing a-way, ye beautiful an - gels, Sing a-way, ye beautiful an - gels,

Singing a - way, Singing a - way, Glory, glory to the Lamb.

Singing a - way, Singing a - way, Glory, glory to the Lamb.

Singing a - way, Singing a - way, Glory, glory to the Lamb.

Sing a - way, Sing a - way, Glory, glory to the Lamb.

OPENING LAY.

Welcome, welcome, welcome! We welcome you, dear friends, in

Welcome, welcome, welcome! We welcome you, dear friends, in

this our op'ning lay; Welcome, welcome, welcome; Welcome here this festal day!

this our op'ning lay; Welcome, welcome, welcome! Welcome here this festal day;

Duet. Moderato.

1st Treble.

1. Many are the sorrows, many are the tears, Many are the hopes, and
2. Many joys we've tasted, many hopes have fled, Many friends are number'd
3. Many are the dangers, many are the snares, Many are the conflicts,

2d Treble.

many are the fears That have cross'd our pathway since we last did meet;
with the si - lent dead, Since last we met to cel - e-brate this day;
many are the cares, That the Lord has kind-ly led his people through,

D. C.

But we've come a - gain, our kin - dred and our friends to greet.
But we've come a - gain, to greet you with our cheer - ful lay.
And a - gain in peace we cel - e-brate this day with you.

D. C.

F

SOUND THE BATTLE CRY!

Words and Music by Wm. F. Sherwin.

March time.

1. Sound the battle cry! See! the foe is nigh; Raise the standard high For the Lord;

2. Strong to meet the foe, Marching on we go, While our cause we know Must prevail;

3. Oh! thou God of all, Hear us when we call; Help us one and all By thy grace;

Gird your armor on, Stand firm every one; Rest your cause upon his ho-ly word.

Shield and banner bright, Gleaming in the light; Battling for the right We ne'er can fail.

When the battle's done, And the vict'ry won, May we wear the crown Before thy face

Rouse, then, soldiers! rally round the banner! Ready, steady, pass the word along;

Chorus.

Rouse, then, soldiers! rally round the banner! Ready, steady, pass the word along;

Onward, forward, Shout aloud hosannah! Christ is Captain of the mighty throng.

Onward, forward, Shout aloud hosannah! Christ is Captain of the mighty throng.

OVER THERE.

T. C. O'KANE.

1. O, think of a home over there, By the side of the river of light, Where the

2. O, think of the friends over there, Who before us the journey have trod, Of the

3. My Saviour is now over there, There my kindred and friends are at rest; Then a-
4. I'll soon be at home over there, For the end of my journey I see; Many

saints all immortal and fair, Are robed in their garments of white, over there.

songs that they breathe on the air, In their home in the palace of God, over there.

way from my sorrow and care, Let me fly to the land of the blest, over there.
dear to my heart over there, Are watching and waiting for me, over there.

Over there, over there, O, think of a home over there,

Over there, over there, O, think of the friends over there, over there.

Over there, over there, My Saviour is now over there, over there.
Over there, over there, I'll soon be at home over there, over there.

Over there, o - ver there, o - ver there, O think of a home over there.

Over there, over there, O, think of the friends over there.

O-ver there, over there, over there, My Saviour is now o - ver there.
O-ver there, over there, over there, I'll soon be at rest o - ver there.

O - ver there.

SAFE WITHIN THE VAIL.

J. M. Evans.

Three beats to the measure.

1. Land a - head!" Its fruits are waving   O'er the hills of fadeless green;

2. Onward, bark! the cape I'm rounding;   See the blessed wave their hands;

3. There, let go   the an - chor, riding   On this calm and silv'ry   bay;
4. Now we're safe from all temptation,   All the storms of life are   past;

And the liv - ing waters   laving Shores where heav'nly forms are seen.

Hear the harps of God re-sound-ing From the bright im-mor-tal   bands.

Seaward fast   the tide is gliding,   Shores in sun - light stretch a - way.
Praise the Rock of our sal - va - tion, We are safe   at home at   last!

Chorus.

Rocks and storms I'll fear no more, When on   that   e-ter-nal   shore;

Rocks and storms I'll fear no more, When on   that   e-ter-nal   shore;

Drop the an-chor! Furl the   sail!   I   am   safe   within   the   vail!

Drop the an-chor! Furl the   sail!   I   am   safe   within   the   vail!

WHEN THE MORNING LIGHT.

Rev. R. Lowry.

1 When the morn-ing light drives away the night, With the sun so bright and full,
And the day of rest light-ens every breast; I'll a - way to the Sabbath-School,

2 On the fros-ty dawn of a win-ter's morn, When the earth is wrapp'd in snow,
Or the sum-mer breeze plays around the trees, to the Sab-bath-School I go;

For 'tis there we all a-gree, All with hap-py hearts and free, And I

When the ho-ly day has come And the Sab-bath break-ers roam, I de-love to ear-ly be At the Sab-bath-School: I'll a-way! a-way! I'll a

GIRLS. BOYS. GIRLS.

light to leave my home For the Sabbath-School: I'll a-way! a-way! I'll a

way! away! I'll away! to Sabbath-School

BOYS. ALL.

way! away! I'll away! to Sabbath-School.

3. In the class I meet with the friends I greet,
At the time of morning prayer;
And our hearts we raise in a hymn of praise
For ,tis always pleasant there.
In the Book of holy truth,
Full of counsel and reproof,
We behold the guide of youth,
At the Sabbath-School:
I'll away! &c.

4. May the dews of grace fill the hallow'd place
And the sunshine never fail,
While each blooming rose which in memory grows,
Shall a sweet perfume exhale.
When we mingle here no more,
But have met on Jordan's shore,
We will talk of moments o'er,
At the Sabbath-School:
I'll away! &c.

3

PRAISE! GIVE PRAISE.

FANNY CROSBY.　　　　　　　　　　　　CHESTER G. ALLEN.

1. Praise him, praise him, Je-sus, our blessed Re-deem - er, Sing, O earth, his

2. Praise him, praise him, Je-sus, our blessed Re-deem - er, For our sins he

3. Praise him, praise him, Je-sus, our blessed Re-deem - er, Heav'nly por - tals,

wonderful love pro-claim. Hail him, hail him, highest archangels in glo-ry,
D. S. O ye saints, that dwell on the mountain of Zion,

suffered and bled and died; He, our rock, our hope of e - ter - nal sal - vation.
D. S. Once for us re - ject-ed, despised, and forsaken,

loud with hosannahs ring, Je - sus, Saviour, reigneth for-ev - er and ev - er;
D. S. Jesus lives! No longer thy portals are cheerless;

Strength and hon-or give to his ho - ly name. Like a shep - herd
Praise him, praise him ev - er in joy - ful song.

Fine.

Hail him, hail him, Je - sus, the cru - ci - fied. Lov - ing Sa - viour,
Prince of Glo - ry, He is tri - um-phant now.

Fine.

Crown him, crown him Prophet, and Priest, and King. Death is vanquished!
Je - sus lives, the mighty and strong to save.

Jesus will guard his children, In his arms he carried them all day long. D. S.

meekly en-dur-ing sorrow, Crown'd with thorns that cruelly pierced his brow. D. S.

Tell it with joy ye faithful. Where is now thy vic - to - ry, boasting grave? D. S.

LOVE AT HOME. 7s & 5s.

J. H. McNaughton.

1. There is beauty all around, When there's love at home; There is joy in ev'ry sound,

2. In the cottage there is joy, When there's love at home; Hate and envy ne'er annoy,

3. Kindly heav'n smiles above, When there's love at home; All the earth is filled with love,
4. Jesus make me wholly thine, Then there's love at home; May thy sacrifice be mine,

When there's love at home. Peace and plenty here abide, Smiling sweet on ev'ry side,

When there's love at home. Roses blossom 'neath our feet, All the earth's a garden sweet,

When there's love at home. Sweeter sings the brooklet by, Brighter beams the azure sky;
Then there's love at home. Safely from all harm I'll rest, With no sinful care distress'd,

Time doth softly sweetly glide, When there's love at home, Love at home,

Making life a bliss complete, When there's love at home, Love at home,

Oh, there's One who smiles on high When there's love at home, Love at home,
Thro' thy tender mercy blessed, With thy love at home.   Love at home,

love at home, Time doth softly, sweetly glide, When there's love at home.

love at home, Time doth softly, sweetly glide, When there's love at home.

THE WATER OF LIFE.

W. B. Bradbury.

1. Je - sus the wa - ter of life will give, Free - ly, free - ly, free - ly,
   Come to that fountain, oh, drink and live, Free - ly, free - ly, free - ly,

2. Je - sus has promised a home in heav'n, Free - ly, free - ly, free - ly,
   Treasures un-fad - ing will there be given, Free - ly, free - ly, free - ly,

3. Je - sus has promised a robe of white, Free - ly, free - ly, free - ly,
   Kingdoms of glo - ry, and crowns of light, Free - ly, free - ly, free - ly,

1st. 2d.

Je - sus the wa-ter of life will give, Freely to those who love him.)
Come to that fountain, oh, drink and live, Flowing for those that - - - } love him.

Jesus has promis'd a home in heav'n, Freely to those that love him.)
Treasures unfading will there be given, Freely to those that - - - } love him.

Jesus has promis'd a robe of white, Freely to those that love him.)
Kingdoms of glory, and crowns of light, Freely to those that - - - } love him.

The Spi - rit and the Bride say, come, Free-ly, free - ly, free - ly, And

The Spi - rit and the Bride say, come, Free - ly, free - ly, free - ly, And

he that is thirsty let him come, And drink of the wa - ter of life.

he that is thirsty let him come, And drink of the wa - ter of life.

4. Jesus has promised eternal day,
    Freely, freely, freely,
Jesus has promised eternal day,
    Freely to those that love him;
Pleasure that never shall pass away,
    Freely, freely, freely,
Pleasure that never shall pass away,
    Freely to those that love him.

5. Jesus has promised a calm repose,
    Freely, freely, freely,
Jesus has promised a calm repose,
    Freely to all that love him;
Come to the water of life that flows,
    Freely, freely, freely,
Come to the water of life that flows,
    Freely to all that love him.

THE WATER OF LIFE. Concluded.

Chorus.

The fountain of life is flow - ing, Flow - ing, free - ly flow - ing,

The fountain of life is flow - ing, Flow - ing, free - ly flow - ing,

The fountain of life is flow - ing, Is flowing for you and for me.

The fountain of life is flow - ing, Is flowing for you and for me.

1. There is no name so sweet on earth, No name so sweet in heaven, }
The name before his wondrous birth To Christ, the Saviour   } given.

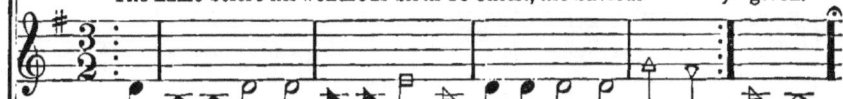

2. His human name they did proclaim, When Abram's son they seal'd him : }
The name that still by God's good will, De - liv - er - er   re-   } veal'd him.

D. C. For there's no word ear ev - er heard, So dear, so sweet, as   Je - sus.

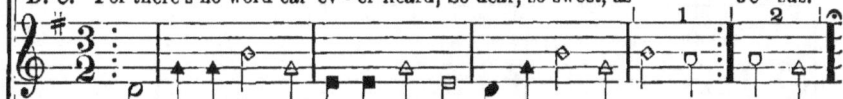

3. And when he hung up-on the tree, They wrote his name above him, }
That all might see the reason we For - ev - er-more must   •   } love him.

4. So   now up - on his Father's throne, Almighty to   re - lease us }
From sin and pains, he gladly reigns, The Prince and Saviour,   } Je - sus.

Chorus.   *D. C.*

We love   to   sing   around   our King, And hail him bless - ed   Je - sus;

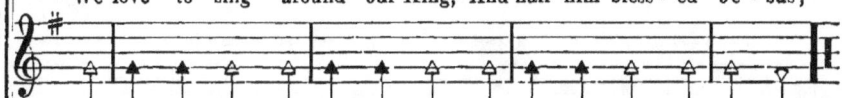

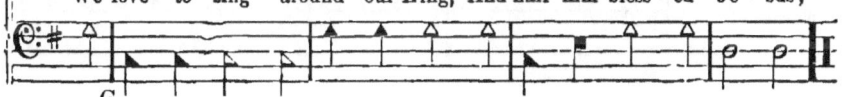

D. C.

We love   to   sing   around   our King, And hail him bless - ed   Je - sus;

G

THE SABBATH-SCHOOL.

Wm. B. Bradbury.

1. The Sabbath-school's a place of pray'r: I love to meet my teachers there, I love to meet my

2. In God's own book we're taught to read, How Christ for sinners groan'd and bled, How Christ for sinne

3. In Sabbath-school we sing and pray, And learn to love the Sabbath day, And learn to love the

4. And when our days on earth are o'er, We'll meet in heav'n to part no more, We'll meet in heav'n t

teachers there; They teach me there that ev'ry one May find in heav'n a happy home, May

groan'd and bled; That precious blood a ransom gave For sin-ful man, his soul to save, For

Sabbath day; That, when on earth our Sabbaths end, A glorious rest in heav'n we'll spend, A

part no more; Our teachers kind we there shall greet, And oh! what joy 'twill be to meet, And find   in heav'n   a   hap - py home.   I   love   to   go,   I

sin - ful man,   his soul to   save.   I   love   to   go,   I

Boys.   All.

glo - rious rest   in heav'n we'll spend. I   love to   go,   I love to   go,   I

oh!   what joy   'twill be to   meet In heav'n a - bove, In heav'n a - bove, In

love to go to Sabbath-school, I   love to go, I   love to go, I love to go to Sabbath-school.

love to go to Sabbath-school, I   love to go, I   love to go, I   love to go to Sabbath-school.

Boys.   All.

love to go to Sabbath-school, I   love to go, I love to go, I love to go to Sabbath-school.

heav'n above, to part no more, In heav'n above, in heav'n above, In heav'n above, to part no more!

I LOVE TO TELL THE STORY.

Wm. G. Fischer.

1. I love to tell the sto - ry Of unseen things a- bove, Of Je -sus and his glo- ry,
2. I love to tell the sto - ry: More wonderful it seems Than all the golden fancies

3. I love to tell the sto - ry: 'Tis pleasant to repeat, What seems each time I tell it,
4. I love to tell the sto - ry; For those who know it best, Seem hungering and thirsting

Of Je-sus and his love. I love to tell the sto-ry, Because I know its true;
Of all our gold- en dreams. I love to tell the sto-ry: It did so much for me!

More won-der-ful - ly sweet. I love to tell the sto-ry: For some have never heard
To hear it like the rest. And when in scenes of glory, I sing the New, New Song,

It sa-tis-fies my longings, As nothing else would do.   I love to tell the sto-ry, 'Twill
And that is just the reason I tell it now to thee.   I love to tell the sto-ry, 'Twill

The message of sal-va-tion From God's own holy word. I love to tell the   sto-ry, 'Twill
'Twill be—the OLD, OLD STORY That I have loved so long! I love to tell the   sto-ry, 'Twill

be my theme in glo-ry to tell the old,   old   story, Of Jesus and his love.

be my theme in glory, to tell the old,   old   sto-ry, of Je-sus and his love.

"LOOKING HOME."

Steady movement, nearly as in 4—4 time.

1. Ah! this heart is void and chill, 'Mid earth's noisy throngings; For my Father's

2. Soon the glorious day will dawn, Heav'nly pleasures bringing; Night will be ex-

3. Oh! to be at home a-gain, All for which we're sighing, From all earthly

4. With this load of sin and care, Then no long-er bending, But with waiting
5. Blessed home, oh! blessed home, All for which we're sighing; Soon our Lord will

Chorus.

mansions still Ear-nest-ly is long-ing. Look-ing home, Looking home,

changed for morn, Sighs give place to sing-ing. Look-ing home, Looking home,

want and pain To be swift-ly fly-ing! Look-ing home, Looking home,

an - gels there On our soul at-tend-ing. Look-ing home, Looking home,
bid us come To our Fa-ther's king-dom. Look-ing home, Looking home,

Towards the heav'nly mansions Jesus hath prepared for me, In his Father's kingdom.

Towards the heav'nly mansions Jesus hath prepared for me, In his Father's kingdom.

Towards the heav'nly mansions Jesus hath prepared for me, In his Father's kingdom.

THE SAVIOUR CALLS.

1. To - day the Saviour calls: Ye wand'rers, come; O ye benighted souls, Why longer roam?

2. To - day the Saviour calls: Oh, hear him now; Within these sacred walls To Je-sus bow.

3. To - day the Saviour calls: For refuge fly; The storm of justice falls, And death is nigh.
4. The Spirit calls to - day: Yield to his pow'r; Oh, grieve him not a-way; 'Tis mercy's hour.

WHITE ROBES.

1. Who are these in bright ar - ray, This ex - ult - ing, hap-py throng, Round the
2. These thro' fi - ery tri - als trod, These from great afflic - tions came; Now be-

3. Clad in rai-ment pure and white, Vic-tor palms in eve-ry hand, Through their
4. Joy and gladness ban-ish sighs; Perfect love dis-pels all fears; And for-

Chorus.

al - tar night and day, Singing one triumphant song? They have clean robes, white robes,
fore the throne of God, Seal'd with his al-migh-ty name.

great Redeemer's might, More than conquerors they stand. They have clean robes, white robes,
ev - er from their eyes, God shall wipe away their tears.

White robes are waiting for me! Yes, clean robes, white robes, Wash'd in the blood of the Lamb.

White robes are waiting for me! Yes, clean robes, white robes, Wash'd in the blood of the Lamb.

MORN OF ZION'S GLORY.

1. Morn of Zi-on's glo - ry, Brightly thou art breaking, Ho - ly joy thy light a-waking;

2. Morn of Zi-on's glo - ry, Eve-ry human dwelling With thy notes of joy is swelling;

3. Morn of Zi-on's glo - ry, Now the night is riv - en; Now the star is high in heaven;

MORN OF ZION'S GLORY.

Morn of Zion's glo - ry,   Ancient saints foretold thee, Seraph angels glad behold thee:

Morn of Zi-on's glo - ry.   Distant hills are ringing,   Echoed voi-ces sweet are singing,

Morn of Zi-on's glo - ry.   Joy - ful hearts are bounding, Halle-lu -jah sweetly sounding,

Far and wide See them glide; Streams of rich salva - tion Flow   to ev'-ry   na - tion.

Haste thee on, Like the sun, Paths of splendor trac - ing, Hea-then midnight chas-ing.

Peace with men dwells again, Je - sus reigns for-ev - er! Je - sus reigns for-ev - er!

1. There is a hap-py land, Far, far a-way, } Oh, how they sweetly sing,
Where saints in glory stand, Bright, bright as day:

2. Come to this hap-py land, Come, come a-way; } Oh, we shall hap-py be
Why will ye doubting stand? Why still de-lay?

3. Bright in that happy land Beams ev-'ry eve; } Oh, then, to glo-ry run;
Kept by a Father's hand, Love cannot die:

Worthy is our Saviour King, Loud let his prais-es ring, For ev - er more.

When, from sin and sorrow free, Lord, we shall live with thee, Blest ev-er-more.

Be a crown and kingdom won, And bright above the sun Reign ev - er-more.

THE GOOD SHIP ZION.

A. A. G.

1. We are homeward bound to the land of light and love; With a swelling sail we onward sweep;

2. Though the billows rise, they shall never overwhelm, Though the breakers roar upon the lee,

3. Tho' for ages past she has plough'd the stormy main, She's the stout ship Zion as of yore;

4. Ho! ye youthful souls, there is danger in your path; By the chart of folly you're misled:
5. We are homeward bound; won't you join our happy crew? Come aboard, poor sinner, while you may:

Tho' the rude winds blow, there is One who rules above, Who will guard the weary sailor on the deep.

'Mid the strife we'll sing, for we've Jesus at the helm, And he'll steer the good ship Zion o'er the sea.

Safe 'mid rocks and shoals and the fearful hurricane She has thousands brought to Canaan's happy shore.

There are rocks beneath, and above a storm of wrath, And the breakers of destruction are a-head.
To the eye of faith there's the better land in view; 'Tis the land that shines with never-ending day.

In the good ship Zion we are tossing on the tide, But the wild dark tempest soon shall cease;

In the good ship Zion we are tossing on the tide, But the wild dark tempest soon shall cease;

All the danger o - ver, she will safe at anchor ride In the port of ev - er-last-ing peace.

All the danger o - ver, she will safe at anchor ride In the port of ev - er-last-ing peace.

I'LL THINK OF MY SAVIOUR.

Wm. B. Bra [ry.]

1. I'll think of my Sa - viour when day - light is break - ing A-
When fresh from his slum - bers tho sun is a - wak - ing, And

2. I'll think of my Sa - viour when day - light is sink - ing, And
When bright star - ry eyes in the a - zure are twink - ling, And

3. I'll think of my Sa - viour when plea - sure is spread - ing Her
Through sor-row and sad - ness, a - lone he was tread - ing, To

4. I'll think of my Sa - viour when sor - row is fling - ing Her
If light from his pre - sence a glo - ry is bring - ing, 'Twill

5. I'll think of my Sa - viour, my dear, bless - ed Sa - viour, When
And take to his bo - som his loved ones for - ev - er, To

way from the darkness and gloom of the night, ... ar - mor of light. }
gird - ing him - self with the . . . . ar - mor of light. }

blend-ing its beams with the twi - light so gray, ... close of the day. }
si - lence em - bra - ces the . . . . close of the day. }

soft down - y pin - ions to glad - den my way; . . . . por - tals of day. }
o - pen for sin - ners the . . . . por - tals of day. }
thick robe of sad - ness a - round the dark tomb; . . . . hide all its gloom. }
scat - ter its dark - ness and . . . . hide all its gloom. }

he from on high his bright an - gels shall send . . . . nev - er shall end. }
join in the an - thems that . . . . nev - er shall end. }

Chorus. **Girls.** **Boys.** **Both.**

I'll think of my Sa - viour, And trust him for - ev - er. I'll

I'll think of my Sa - viour, And trust him for - ev - er. I'll

I'll think of my Sa - viour, And trust him for - ev - er. I'll

seek for his fa - vor, And hope, through his love, With an - gels to meet him, With

seek for his fa - vor, And hope, through his love, With an - gels to meet him, With

seek for his fa - vor, And hope, through his love, With an - gels to meet him, With ser - aphs to greet him, And praise him for - ov - er In man-sions a - bove.

ser - aphs to greet him, And praise him for - ev - er In man-sions a - bove.

ser - aphs to greet him, And praise him for - ev - er In man-sions a - bove.

PEACEFULLY SLEEP.

Slow.

1. Peacefully lay her down to rest, Place the turf kindly on her breast;

2. Close to her lone and nar - row house, Gracefully wave, ye wil-low boughs;

3. Qui - et - ly sleep, be - lov - ed one; Rest from thy toil—thy labor is done;

Sweet is thy slumber beneath the sod, While the pure soul is resting with God.

Flowers of the wildwood, your odors shed Over the ho - ly, beautiful dead.

Rest till the trump from the opening skies Bid thee from dust to glo-ry a - rise!

Peacefully sleep, Peacefully sleep, Sleep till that morning, Peacefully sleep.

Peacefully sleep, Peacefully sleep, Sleep till that morning, Peacefully sleep.

Peacefully sleep, Peacefully sleep, Sleep till that morning, Peacefully sleep.

Spirited.

1. We journey on to the land above, A land of light and a land of love;

2. A lit-tle while in the land below, To that above we will short-ly go;

3. And while we pass through the land below, We'll look to that where we soon shall go,

4. When life is done, and its conflict past, The land above we will gain at last,

We're strangers here, and the land we're in, Tho' a pleasant land, is a land of sin.

A few more days on the pilgrim road, Then we'll rest at home with the Lord our God.

And fix our eyes on our Saviour's throne: We must seek for strength in his grace alone.

And shout for joy as we en-ter in, Fare-well, farewell to the land of sin!

Chorus.

We are jour-ney-ing on to the land of Canaan, Trav'ling with saints to the

We are jour-ney-ing on to the land of Canaan, Trav'ling with saints to the

Chorus to last verse.

We are here, safe-ly here, in the land of Canaan, Dwell-ing with saints in the

blissful haven ; There we shall dwell, there we shall dwell, Ever in the land of Canaan.

blissful haven ; There we shall dwell, there we shall dwell, Ever in the land of Canaan.

blissful haven ; Here we shall dwell, here we shall dwell, Ever in the land of Canaan.

THE EVERGREEN SHORE.

Words by Wm. Hunter, D.D.

Wm. B. Bradbury.

1. We are joy-ous-ly voy-ag-ing o-ver the main, Bound for the ev-er-green

2. We have nothing to fear from the wind and the wave, Under our Saviour's com-

3. Both the winds and the waves our Commander controls; Nothing can baf-fle his
4. In the thick, murky night, when the stars and the moon Send not a glimmering

5. Let the high-heaving billow, and mountainous wave, Fearful-ly o-ver-head
6. Let the vessel be wreck'd on the rock or the shoal, Sink to be seen nev-er-

shore, Whose inhab-it-ants never of sickness complain, And never see death any

mand; And our hearts in the midst of the dangers are brave; For Jesus will bring us to

skill; And his voice, when the thundering hurricane rolls, Can make the loud tempest be
ray, Then the light of his countenance, brighter than noon, Will drive all our terror a-

break; There is One by our side that can comfort and save; There's One that will never for-
more; He will bear, none the less, ev'ry passenger soul, Safe, safe to the ev-ergreen

Chorus.

more. Then let the hur-ri-cane roar, It will the soon-er be o'er;

' land. Then let the hur-ri-cane roar, It will the soon-er be o'er;

still. Then let the hur-ri-cane roar, It will the soon-er be o'er;
way.

sake.
shore.

We will weather the blast, and will land at last Safe on the ev-er-green shore.

We will weather the blast, and will land at last Safe on the ev-er-green shore.

We will weather the blast, and will land at last Safe on the ev-er-green shore.

THE BEAUTIFUL RIVER.

Rev. R. Lowry.

Spirited.

1. Shall we gath-er at the riv-er, Where bright an-gel feet have trod,

2. On the mar-gin of the riv-er, Washing up its sil-ver spray,

3. On the bo-som of the riv-er, Where the Saviour-King we own,
4. Ere we reach the shining riv-er, Lay we ev'-ry bur-den down;

5. At the smil-ing of the riv-er, Rippling with the Saviour's face,
6. Soon we'll reach the shining riv-er, Soon our pil-grim-age will cease;

With its crys-tal tide for-ev-er Flowing by the throne of God?

We will walk and worship ev-er All the hap-py, gold-en day.

We shall meet, and sor-row nev-er, 'Neath the glo-ry of the throne,
Grace our spi-rits will de-liv-er And pro-vide a robe and crown.

Saints, whom death will never sev-er, Lift their songs of sav-ing grace.
Soon our hap-py hearts will quiv-er With the mel-o-dy of peace.

Chorus.

Yes, we'll gather at the riv-er, The beau-ti-ful, the beau-ti-ful riv-er—

Yes, we'll gather at the riv-er, The beau-ti-ful, the beau-ti-ful riv-er—

Yes, we'll gather at the riv-er, The beau-ti-ful, the beau-ti-ful riv-er—

Gather with the saints at the riv-er That flows by the throne of God.

Gather with the saints at the riv-er That flows by the throne of God.

Gather with the saints at the riv-er That flows by the throne of God.

THE PURE IN HEART.

Words by KATE CAMERON.   W. B. BRADBURY.

1. Bless - ed   are   the   pure   in   heart!   Bless - ed   ev - er - more!
They shall meet, and   nev - er   part   On   the   gol - den   shore.

2. Bless - ed   are   the   pure   in   heart!   Free from   sin   and   stain;
Sa - tan   with   his   fi - ery   dart, Tempts their peace   in   vain;

3. Bless - ed   are   the   poor   in   heart,   Oh!   that   we   may   stand,
Choos - ing   now   the   bet - ter   part,   At   the Lord's right hand.

Thorn - y paths their   feet have trod, But their rest is   sure with God.

For they   lean   on   Je - sus's arm, He will keep them safe from harm.

With us   may   His   love a - bide, For the sake of Christ who died!

Chorus.

Bless - ed are the pure in heart, Bless - ed ev - er - more;

Bless - ed are the pure in heart, Bless - ed ev - er - more.

Bless - ed are the pure in heart, Bless - ed ev - er - more.

Bless - ed are the pure in heart, Bless - ed ev - er - more.

1. A beau-ti-ful land by faith I see, A land of rest, from sorrow free,

2. That beautiful land, the City of Light, It ne'er has known the shades of night;

3. In vi-sion I see its streets of gold, Its beau-ti-ful gates I too be-hold,

4. The hea-ven-ly throng array'd in white, In rapture range the plains of light;

The home of the ransom'd, bright and fair, And beauti-ful angels, too, are there.

The glo-ry of God, the light of day, Hath driven the darkness far a-way.

The riv-er of life, the crys-tal sea, The am-bro-sial fruit of life's fair tree.

And in one harmonious choir they praise Their glorious Saviour's matchless grace.

Chorus.

Will you go? Will you go? Go to that beau-ti-ful land with me?

Will you go? Will you go? Go to that beau-ti-ful land with me?

Will you go? Will you go? Go to that beau-ti-ful land?

Will you go? Will you go? Go to that beau-ti-ful land?

BEAUTIFUL LAND ON HIGH.

W. U. BUTCHER.

1. There's a beau-ti-ful land on high, To its glo-ries I fain would fly,

2. There's a beau-ti-ful land on high, I shall en-ter it by-and-by,

3. There's a beau-ti-ful land on high, Then why should I fear to die,
4. There's a beau-ti-ful land on high, And my kindred its bliss en-joy;

5. There's a beau-ti-ful land on high, Where I never shall weep or sigh;
6. There's a beau-ti-ful land on high, Where we never shall say "good-bye;"

When by sorrows press'd down I long for my crown In that beautiful land on high.

There with friends hand in hand I shall walk on the strand, In that beautiful land on high.

When death is the way to the realms of day, In that beautiful land on high?
And methinks I now see them waiting for me, In that beautiful land on high.

For my Father hath said no tear shall be shed In that beautiful land on high.
Where the righteous will sing, and their chorus will ring In that beautiful land on high.

In that beau-ti-ful land I'll be From earth and its cares set free; My

In that beau-ti-ful land I'll be From earth and its cares set free; My

In that beau-ti-ful land I'll be From earth and its cares set free; My

Je - sus is there, He's gone to prepare A place in that land for me.

Je - sus is there, He's gone to prepare A place in that land for me.

Je - sus is there, He's gone to prepare A place in that land for me.

"JUST NOW."

Come to Je - sus, Come to Je - sus, Come to Je - sus just now;

Come to Je - sus, Come to Je - sus, Come to Je - sus just now;

Just now come to Je - sus, Come to Je - sus just now.

Just now come to Je - sus, Come to Je - sus just now.

1. Come to Jesus just now, &c.

"Come unto me, all ye that labor and are heavy laden, and I will give you rest."—*Matt.* 11 : 28.

2. He will save you, just now, &c.

"Believe on the Lord Jesus Christ, and thou shalt be saved."—*Acts* 16 : 31.

3. O believe him, just now, &c.

"God so loved the world that he gave his only begotten Son, that whosoever believeth in him should not perish, but have everlasting life."—*John* 3 : 16.

4. He is able.

"He is able to save them to the uttermost that come unto God by him, seeing he ever liveth to make intercession for them."—*Heb.* 7 : 25.

5. He is willing.

"The Lord is long suffering to usward, not willing that any should perish, but that all should come to repentance."—*2 Pet.* 3 : 9.

6. He'll receive you.

"Him that cometh to me, I will in no wise cast out."—*John* 6 : 37.

7. Then flee to Jesus.

"Flee from the wrath to come."—*Matt.* 3 : 7.

8. Call unto him.

"Whosoever shall call on the name of the Lord shall be saved."—*Acts* 2 : 21.

9. "Mercy on me."

"Jesus, thou son of David, have mercy on me."—*Mark* 10 : 47.

10. He will hear you.

"And Jesus said unto him, Go thy way, thy faith hath made thee whole."—*Mark* 10 : 52.

11. He'll forgive you.

"If we confess our sins, he is faithful and just to forgive us our sins."—*1 John* 1 : 9.

12. He will cleanse you.

"The blood of Jesus Christ his Son, cleanseth us from all sin."—*1 John* 1 : 7.

13. He'll renew you.

"Therefore, if any man be in Christ, he is a new creature."—*2 Cor.* 5 : 17.

14. He will clothe you.

"He that overcometh, the same shall be clothed in white raiment."—*Rev.* 3 : 5.

15. Jesus loves you.

"Greater love hath no man than this, that a man should lay down his life for his friends."—*John* 15 : 13.

16. Don't reject him.

"He is despised and rejected of men."—*Isa.* 53 : 3.

17. Only trust him.

"He that hath the Son hath life."—*John* 5 : 12.

This little Chorus has been the means of helping many an inquiring sinner to embrace the Saviour, believe and trust him. "It was," says Rev. Mr. Hammond, "first sung in Scotland, when hundreds were asking, 'What shall we do to be saved?'"

128   THE SHINING SHORE.

George F. Root.

1. My days are glid-ing swift-ly by, And I, a pilgrim stranger, Would

2. We'll gird our loins, my brethren dear, Our heav'nly home discerning; Our

3. Should coming days be cold and dark, We need not cease our sing-ing; That

4. Let sorrow's rud-est tem-pest blow, Each chord on earth to sev-er; Our

no' de-tain them as they fly, Those hours of toil and dan-ger.

ab-sent Lord has left us word, Let ev'-ry lamp be burn-ing.

per-fect rest naught can mo-lest, Where gold-en harps are ring-ing.

King says, Come, and there's our home, For-ev-er, oh! for-ev-er!

Chorus.

For, oh! we stand on Jordan's strand, Our friends are passing o - ver, And

For, oh! we stand on Jordan's strand, Our friends are passing o - ver, And

For, oh! we stand on Jordan's strand, Our friends are passing o - ver, And

just be - fore, the shining shore We may al - most dis - cov - er.

HAPPY DAY.

Arranged by H. WATERS.

1. Preserved by thine Al-migh-ty power, O Lord, our Maker, Saviour, King,
And brought to see this happy hour, We come thy praises here to sing.

2. We praise thee for thy constant care, For life preserved, for mercies giv'n:
Oh, may we still those mercies share, And taste the joys of sins forgiv'n.

3. We praise thee for the joy-ful news Of pardon through a Saviour's blood:
O Lord, in-cline our hearts to choose The road to hap - pi-ness and God.

4. And when on earth our days are done, Grant, Lord, that we at length may join,
Teachers and scholars, round thy throne, The song of Moses and the Lamb.

Chorus.

Hap - py day, Hap - py day! Here in thy courts we'll glad - ly stay,

Hap - py day, Hap - py day! Here in thy courts we'll glad - ly stay,

Hap - py day, Hap - py day! Here in thy courts we'll glad - ly stay,

And at thy foot- stool humbly pray That thou wouldst take our sins a - way.

And at thy foot - stool humbly pray That thou wouldst take our sins a - way.

And at thy foot- stool humbly pray That thou wouldst take our sins a - way.

Hap - py day, hap - py day, When Christ shall wash our sins a - way!

Hap - py day, hap - py day, When Christ shall wash our sins a - way!

Hap - py day, hap - py day, When Christ shall wash our sins a - way!

HARK! THE VOICE OF JESUS.

Words by V. A.

P. P. Van Arsdale.

1. Hark! the voice of Je - sus calling, Who will go and work to-day?

2. If you cannot cross the o - cean, And the heathen lands explore,

3. If you cannot speak like an-gels; If you cannot preach like Paul;
4. While the souls of men are dying, And the Mas-ter calls for you,

Fields are white, the har - vest wait-ing, Who will bear the sheaves a - way?

You can find the heathen nearer, You can help them at your door;

You can tell the love of Je-sus, You can say he died for all;
Let none hear you i - dly saying, "There is nothing I can do!

Loud and long the Mas - ter calleth, Rich reward he of - fers free;

If you can - not give your thousands, You can give the widow's mite,

If you fail to rouse the wicked, With the judgment's dread a - larms,
Glad - ly take the task he gives you; Let his work his pleasure be;

Who will an - swer, glad - ly say - ing, "Here am I, O Lord, send me."

And the least you do for Je - sus Will be precious in his sight.

You may lead the lit - tle children To the Saviour's waiting arms.
An - swer quickly when he calleth, "Here am I, O Lord, send me."

WORLD OF LIGHT.

Rev. E. W. Dunbar.

1. There is a beau - ti - ful world, Where saints and an - gels sing,

2. There is a beau - ti - ful world, Where sor-row nev - er comes,

3. There is a beau - ti - ful world, Un - seen by mor - tal sight,

4. There is a beau - ti - ful world, Of har - mo - ny and love:

A world where peace and pleasure reign, And heav'nly praises ring.

A world where tears shall nev-er fall In sigh-ing for our home.

And darkness nev - er en - ters there: That home is fair and bright.

Oh, may we safe - ly en - ter there, And dwell with God a-bove.

Chorus.

We'll be there, We'll be there. Palms of vict' - ry, Crowns of

We'll be there, We'll be there. Palms of vict' - ry, Crowns of

We'll be there, We'll be there. Palms of vict' - ry. Crowns of

Ritard.

glo - ry   we shall wear, In that beau - ti - ful world on high.

glo - ry   we shall wear, In that beau - ti - ful world on high.

glo - ry   we shall wear, In that beau - ti - ful world on high.

FOREVER WITH THE LORD. S. M. (Double.)

L. B. Woodbury.

1. "For-ev - er with the Lord!" Amen. So let it be. Life for the dead is

2. My Fa-ther's house on high, Home of my soul, how near, At times, to Faith's as-

3. Yet doubts still in-ter-vene, And all my com-fort flies; Like Noah's dove, I

in that word, 'Tis im - mor-tal - i - ty. Here, in the body pent,

pi - ring eye, Thy gold - en gates ap-pear! Ah, then my spirit faints

flit between Rough seas and stormy skies: A - non the clouds depart,

Ab - sent from him I roam, Yet night-ly pitch my moving tent A

To reach the land I love; The bright in - her - it - ance of saints, Je-

The winds and wa-ters cease; While sweetly o'er my gladden'd heart Ex-

day's march nearer home, nearer home, nearer home, A day's march nearer home.

ru - sa - lem a-bove, home a-bove, home above, Je - ru - sa - lem a-bove.

pands the bow of peace, bow of peace, bow of peace, Expands the bow of peace.

THE "OCEAN GROVE" SONG.

Words by Rev. E. H. Stokes.   Melody by E. M. Bruce, Har. by Jno. R. Sweeney.

1. Hail thou ev - er roll-ing o - cean, Hail thou ev - er heaving sea,

2. Wi - der than the surging billows, High - er than the silvery waves,

3. See the glory, friends of Je - sus, On this o-cean deep and wide;

Sun - light on thy bo - som gleameth Light and shade al - ter - nate-ly.

Roll the tid-ings of sal - va-tion, Flows the precious blood that saves.

But a glo - ry, clearer, brighter, Lies be - yond this swelling tide.

Chorus.

Far   be-yond the roll-ing bil-lows Lies a ci-ty bright and fair,

Far   beyond the roll-ing bil-lows Lies a ci-ty bright and fair,

Glo-ry to our skil-ful Pi-lot, Soon he'll bring our spirits there.

Glo-ry to our skil-ful Pi-lot, Soon he'll bring our spirits there.

4, Gaze not simply on this ocean,
   Walk not only on the shore,
   Launch ye boldly on its bosom,
   Trust your Pilot evermore.—*Chorus.*

5. Yes, launch out, ye friends of Jesus,
   Spread your sails for that blest shore;
   Praise the Lord, the Pilot's with us,
   We are safe for evermore.—*Chorus.*

"SWEEPING THROUGH THE GATES."

(LAST WORDS OF REV. ALFRED COOKMAN.)

T. C. O'KANE.

1. Who, who are these be-side the chil-ly wave, Just on the bor-ders

2. These, these are they who in their youthful days Found Je-sus ear - ly

3. These, these are they who in affliction's woes Ev - er have found in

4. These, these are they who in the con-flict dire Bold - ly have stood a -

of the silent grave, Shouting Jesus' pow'r to save, Wash'd in the blood of the Lamb.

and in wisdom's ways, Prov'd the fullness of his grace, Wash'd in the blood of the Lamb.

Je-sus calm re-pose, Such as from a pure heart flows, Wash'd in the blood of the Lamb.

mid the hottest fire, Jesus now says, "Come up higher;" Wash'd in the blood of the Lamb.

Chorus.

in the blood of the Lamb

"Sweeping thro' the gates" to the New Jerusalem, "Wash'd in the blood of the Lamb:"

'Sweeping thro' the gates" to the New Jerusalem, "Wash'd in the blood of the Lamb:"

Wash'd in the blood in the blood of the Lamb.

"Sweeping thro' the gates" to the New Jerusalem, "Wash'd in the blood of the Lamb."

"Sweeping thro' the gates" to the New Jerusalem, "Wash'd in the blood of the Lamb."

5. Safe, safe upon the ever-shining shore,
Sin, pain, and death, and sorrow all are o'er;
Happy now and evermore, "Wash'd, &c.
Sweeping through the streets of the New Jerusalem,
"Wash'd in the blood of the Lamb."

6. May we, O Lord, be now entirely thine,
Daily, from sin, be kept by power divine,
Then in heav'n the saints we'll join, "Wash'd, &c.
Sweeping through the streets of the New Jerusalem,
"Wash'd in the blood of the Lamb"

SWEET BY AND BY.

J. P. WEBSTER.

Treble Solo.

1. There's a land that is fair - er than day, And by faith we may see it a - far,
2. We shall sing on that beau-ti-ful shore, The me-lo-di-ous songs of the blest,
3. To our boun - ti-ful Fath-er a - bove We will of - fer the trib-ute of praise,

For the Fa - ther waits ov - er the way, To pre-pare us a dwelling place there.
And our spir - its shall sor-row no more— For a sigh for the bless-ing of rest.
For the glo - ri-ous gift of his love, And the blessings that hallow our days!

Chorus.

by and by, by and by, We shall meet on that beautiful shore, by and by,

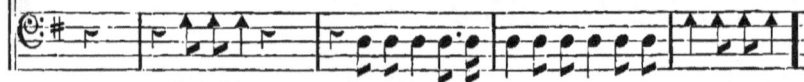

In the sweet by and by, We shall meet on that beautiful shore,

We shall meet on that beautiful shore.

by and by, by and by,

by and by,   by and by, We shall meet on that beau-ti-ful shore.

In the sweet   by and by,   We shall meet on that beau-ti-ful shore.

We shall meet on that beau-ti-ful shore.

by and by,   by and by,

CHANT.—"The Lord is my Shepherd."

DR. L. MASON.

1. The Lord is my shepherd; I|shall not|want.
   He maketh me to lie down in green pastures:
   He leadeth me be-side the|still...|waters.

2. He restoreth my soul: he leadeth me
   In the paths of righteousness for his|name's|
      sake.
   Yea, though I walk through the valley of the
      shadow of death,

I will fear no evil: for thou art with me;
Thy rod and thy staff, they|comfort|me.

3. Thou preparest a table before me in the presence of mine enemies:
   Thou anointest my head with oil; my|cup..
      runeth|over.
   Surely goodness and mercy shall follow me all
      the days of my life;
   And I shall dwell in the house of the|Lord,
   for-|ever, ‖ A-|men.

NEVER GIVE UP THE RIGHT WAY.

Words and Music by GEO. F. ROOT.

Earnestly.

1. Nev-er give up the right way, 'Twill brighten by and by; In eve-ry time of

2. Nev-er give up the right way, Tho' narrow, steep and straight, For at the end is

3. Nev-er give up the right way, Tho' tempted oft and long, Re-mem-ber who is

tri-al The blessed Lord is nigh; Tho' e-vil counsels darken, And ev-il passions try,

shining The Golden Ci-ty's gate, And so, if sorrows darken, And selfish pleasure fly,

near thee, With hand so kind and strong: Whatever then may darken, Whatever fade and die,

Nev-er give up the right way, 'Twill brighten by and by. Nev-er give up,

Nev-er give up the right way, 'Twill brighten by and by. Nev-er give up,

Nev-er give up the right way, 'Twill brighten by and by. Nev-er give up,

Nev-er give up, Nev-er give up the right way, 'Twill brighten by and by.

Nev-er give up, Nev-er give up the right way, 'Twill brighten by and by.

Nev-er give up, Nev-er give up the right way, 'Twill brighten by and by.

AWAY TO THE WOODS.

FOR SUNDAY-SCHOOL PICNIC.

A. A. G.

1. A - way to the woods, a - way, A - way to the woods, a - way!

2. Our flag to the breezes fling, Our flag to the breezes fling,

3. Oh, this is our fes - tal day, Oh, this is our fes - tal day;
4. As free as the air are we, As free as the air are we;

5. We all of us love the school, We all of us love the school;
6. Suc-cess to the school we love, Suc-cess to the school we love!

All nature is smiling, Our young hearts beguiling, Oh, we will be happy to - day.

And, as it waves o'er us, We'll join in the chorus, Till woodland and valley shall ring.

Sweet flow'rets are springing, Sweet songsters are singing, And we will be happy and gay.
Then rally, then rally, From hill-top and valley, And join in our innocent glee.

And 'tis in well-doing We're pleasure pursuing, For truth is our guide and our rule.
It sweetens employment With harmless enjoyment, And trains for the kingdom above.

Chorus.

A-way to the woods, A-way to the woods, Away to the woods, a - way,

A - way, a-way, a-way, a-way, A-way to the woods, a - way,

A - way to the woods, A-way to the woods, Away to the woods, a - way,

A - way, a-way, a - way, a-way, A-way to the woods, a - way!

A - way, a-way, a - way, a-way, A-way to the woods, a - way!

A-way to the woods, A-way to the woods, A-way to the woods, a - way!

BEAUTIFUL CITY.

T. J. C.

1. Beau-ti-ful Zi - on, built a - bove, Beau-ti-ful ci - ty that I love! Beau-ti-ful

2. Beau-ti-ful heav'n, where all is light, Beau-ti-ful an-gels, cloth'd in white; Beautiful

3. Beau-ti-ful crowns on ev'-ry brow, Beau-ti-ful palms the conquerors show; Beautiful

4. Beau-ti-ful throne for Christ our King, Beau-ti-ful songs the angels sing; Beau-ti-ful

gates of pear-ly white, Beau-ti-ful tem-ple— God its light!

strains that nev - er tire, Beau-ti-ful harps thro' all the choir.

robes the ransom'd wear, Beau-ti-ful all who en-ter there.

rest all wanderings cease, Beau-ti-ful home of per-fect peace.

He who was slain on Cal - va - ry, O-pens those pearly gates to me.

There shall I join the cho - rus sweet, Worshiping at the Sa - viour's feet.

Thither I press with ea - ger feet, There shall my rest be long and sweet.

There shall my eyes the Sa - viour see, Haste to this heav'n-ly home with me.

Zi - on, Zi-on, love - ly Zi - on, Beau - ti-ful Zi-on, ci - ty of our God.

Zi - on, Zi - on, love - ly Zi - on, Beau - ti-ful Zi-on, ci - ty of our God.

Zi - on, Zi-on, love - ly Zi - on, Beau - ti-ful Zi - on, ci - ty of our God.

Zi - on, Zi - on, love - ly Zi - on, Beau - ti-ful Zi - on, ci - ty of our God.

FANNY CROSBY.

Ist

1. Strike the harp of Zi - on, wake the tuneful lay; Bear the joy
Lo! the morn is breaking, morn of purest love, - - -

3. O - ver distant regions vail'd in error's night, See the ho -
See! the nations coming at the Saviour's call, - - -

3. Oh, the joyful sto - ry, life to ev' - ry soul! Like a migh
Bringing home the lost ones from the path of sin, - - -

2nd. Time. | **Chorus.**

Praise forev - er, praise to God a - bove. Glo - ry! glo -

Coming now to crown him Lord of all. Glo - ry! glo -:

Till the world shall all be gathered in. Glo - ry! glo -

Glo - ry! glo - ry! hear the e - cho ring! Strike the harp of Zion, wake the tuneful lay;

Glo - ry! glo - ry! hear the e - cho ring! Strike the harp of Zion, wake the tuneful lay;

Glo - ry! glo - ry! hear the e - cho ring! Strike the harp of Zion, wake the tuneful lay;

Bear the joyful tidings far a - way, far away, Bear the joyful tidings far a - way.

Bear the joyful tidings far a - way, far away, Bear the joyful tidings far a - way.

Bear the joyful tidings far a - way, far away, Bear the joyful tidings far a - way.

MY SABBATH HOME.

Words by Dr. C. R. BLACKALL.

W. H. DOANE.
From "Pure Gold." By per.

1. Sweet Sabbath School! more dear to me Than fair-est pal - ace dome,

2. Here first my wil - ful, wand'ring heart, The way of life was shown;

3. Here Je - sus stood with lov - ing voice, En - treating me to come,

My heart e'er turns with joy to thee, My own dear Sabbath Home.

Here first I sought the bet - ter part, And gained a Sabbath Home.

And make of Him my on - ly choice, In this dear Sabbath Home.

Chorus.

Sweet Home! Sweet Home! Sweet Home!

Sabbath Home! Blessed Home! Sabbath Home! Blessed

Sabbath Home! Blessed Home! Sabbath Home! Blessed

Sweet Home! Sweet Home! Sweet Home!

Home! Sweet Home!

Home! My heart e'er turns with joy to thee, My own dear Sabbath Home.

Home! My heart e'er turns with joy to thee, My own dear Sabbath Home.

Home! Sweet Home!

154. I AM THINKING OF HOME.

Words by M. F. KIRBY.   Rev. R. LOWRY.

1. I am thinking of home, of my Father's house, Where the many bright mansons be!
2. I am thinking of home, of the lov'd ones there, Dearest friends who have gone before;

3. I am thinking of home; of my heav'nly home, And my spirit doth long to be,
4. I am thinking of home! yes, of "home, sweet home;" May we all in that home unite.

Of the ci - ty whose streets are all cov - er'd with gold, Of its jas - per walls pure and
With whom we went down to the death-riv-er's side, And so sad - ly thought as we

In the far bet - ter land, where the saints ev - er sing, Of the love of Christ, their Re-
With the white cov-er'd throng, and ex - ult - ing-ly raise, To the tri - une God, sweetest

fair to be - hold, Which the right - eous a - lone ev - er see.
watched by the tide, Of the thrice hap - py morn - ings of yore.

deem - er and King, And of mer - cy so cost - ly, so free.
an - thems of praise, Sing-ing glo - ry, and hon - or, and might.

sweet home,

Oh, home! sweet home! sweet home!   I am thinking, and longing for home;

sweet home,

Be - yond the pearly gate, many mansions wait For the weary ones who journey home.

3.
I am thinking of home; of my heavenly home,
  And my spirit doth long to be,
In that far better land, where the saints ever sing
Of the love of Christ, their Redeemer and King,
  And of mercy, so costly, so free.

4.
I am thinking of home! yes, of "home, sweet home;"
  May we all in that home unite
With the white-covered throng, and exultingly raise
To the triune God, sweetest anthems of praise,
  Singing glory, and honor, and might.

SAFE IN THE ARMS OF JESUS.

W. H. DOANE.

1. Safe in the arms of Je - sus, Safe on His gen - tle breast,

2. Safe in the arms of Je - sus, Safe from corrod - ing care,

3. Je - sus, my heart's dear ref - uge, Je - sus has died for me;

D.C. *Cho. Safe in the arms of Je - sus, Safe on His gen - tle breast,*

FINE.

There by His love o'er- shad - ed, Sweetly my soul shall rest.

Safe from the world's tempta - tions, Sin cannot harm me there. FINE.

Firm on the Rock of A - ges, Ev - er my trust shall be.

There by His love o'er shad - ed, Sweetly my soul shall rest.

Hark! 'tis the voice of an - gels, Borne in a song to me,

Free from the blight of sor - row, Free from my doubts and fears;

Here let me wait with pa - tience, Wait till the night is o'er;

D. C. Chorus.

O - ver the fields of glo - ry, O - ver the Jas - per sea.

On - ly a few more tri - als, On - ly a few more tears.

D. C. Chorus.

Wait till I see the morning Break on the gold - en shore.

DISMISSION. 8s & 7s.

1. Lord dismiss us with thy blessing; Fill our hearts with joy and peace;

2. Thanks we give, and a - do - ra - tion, For thy gos - pel's joyful sound;

Let us each, thy love pos - sess-ing, Tri - umph in re - deeming grace
Oh, re - fresh us, Oh, re - fresh us, Trav'lling through this wil-der-ness.

May the fruits of thy sal - va-tion In our hearts and lives abound.
May thy presence, May thy presence, With us ev - er - more be found.

COME TO JESUS!

Words by Dr. J. B. Peck.

H. P. Main.

1. Come, come to Je - sus! He waits to welcome thee, O wan-d'rer,

2. Come, come to Je - sus! He waits to ran-som thee, O slave, e-

3. Come, come to Je - sus! He waits to light-en thee, O burden'd,

ea - ger - ly; Come, come to Je - sus!

ter - nal - ly; Come, come to Je - sus!

gra-cious - ly; Come, come to Je - sus!

4. Come, come to Jesus!
   He waits to give to thee,
   O blind, a vision free;
   Come, come to Jesus!

5. Come, come to Jesus!
   He waits to shelter thee,
   O weary, blessedly;
   Come, come to Jesus!

6. Come, come to Jesus!
   He waits to carry thee,
   O lamb, so lovingly;
   Come, come to Jesus!

THE PRECIOUS NAME.

Words by LYDIA BAXTER.

W. H. DOANE.
From "Pure Gold." By per.

1. Take the name of Je-sus with you, Child of sor-row and of woe—

2. Take the name of Je-sus ev - er, As a shield from ev'ry snare;

3. Oh! the precious name of Je - sus; How it thrills our souls with joy,
4. At the name of Je-sus bow - ing, Fall-ing prostrate at His feet,

It will joy and comfort give you, Take it, then, where'er you go.

If temptations round you gather, Breathe that ho - ly name in prayer.

When His loving arms re - ceive us, And His songs our tongues employ!
King of kings in heav'n we'll crown Him, When our journey is complete.

Precious name, O how sweet! Hope of earth, and joy of

Precious name, O how sweet! Hope of earth, and joy of

Precious name, O how sweet! Hope of earth, and joy of

Precious name, O how sweet!

heav'n, Precious name, O how sweet, how sweet, Hope of earth, and joy of heav'n.

heav'n, Precious name, O how sweet! Hope of earth, and joy of heav'n.

heav'n, Precious name, O how sweet! Hope of earth, and joy of heav'n.

1. Oh, come, let us sing! Our youthful hearts now swelling, To God a-bove, a

2. The full notes pro-long; Our fes - tal cel - e - brat-ing, We hail the day with

God of love, Oh, come, let us sing! Our joy - ful spir-its glad and free, With

cheer-ful lay, And full notes prolong. Both cheerful youth and silv'ry age, And high e - mo-tions rise to thee, In heav'nly mel - o - dy: Oh, come, let us sing!

childhood pure, the gay, the sage, These thrilling scenes engage, Full notes to prolong.

3. Oh, swell, swell the song,
   His praises oft repeating:
   His Son he gave our souls to save:
     Oh, swell, swell the song.
   The humble heart's devotion bring,
   Whence gushing streams of love do spring,
   And make the welkin ring
     With sweet-swelling song.

4. We'll chant, chant his praise,
   Our lofty strains now blending,—
   A tribute bring to Christ our King,
     And chant, chant his praise!
   Our Saviour-Prince was crucified,
   "'Tis finish'd," then he meekly cried,
   And bow'd his head and died:
     Then chant, chant his praise!

5. All full chorus join!
   To Jesus condescending
   To bless our race with heav'nly grace,
     A full chorus join!
   To God, whose mercy on us smiled,
   And Holy Spirit, reconciled
   By Christ, the meek and mild,
     All full chorus join!

HAPPY HOME.

W. H. DOANE.

Words by Miss J. POLLARD.

From "Pure Gold." By per.

1. To the humble soul that is born anew, And from death to life hath past.

2. By the precious blood of our ris-en Lord, When the storm-cloud darkly lowers.

3. If we live by faith, like the pure and just, When the night of death is past.

What a glorious hope of a coming rest, And a home in heaven at last.

We can look a-bove with the eye of faith, And be-lieve that home is ours.

We shall wake with God in that blest a-bode, And our crowns before him cast.

Chorus.

Do we long to fly a-way, To those reams of end-less day, Nev-er,

Do we long to fly a-way, To those reams of end-less day, Nev-er,

Do we long to fly a-way, To those reams of end-less day, Nev-er,

nev-er more to stray from our Hap-py Home, Happy Home,

nev-er more to stray from our Happy Home, Hap-py Home, Hap-py

nev-er more to stray from our Happy Home, Hap-py Home, Hap-py

Happy Home,

HAPPY HOME. Concluded.

Happy Home,   Blest abode, where the   Saviour dwells,

Home,   Blest a - bode,   where the   Saviour dwells, Happy

Home,   Blest a - bode,   where the   Saviour dwells, Happy

Happy Home,   Blest abode, where the   Saviour dwells,

Happy Home,   Happy Home, Blest abode, where the Saviour dwells.

Home,   Happy Home,   Blest abode, where the Saviour dwells.

Home,   Happy Home,   Blest adode, where the Saviour dwells.

Happy Home,   Happy Home, Blest abode, where the Saviour dwells.

GATHER THEM INTO THE FOLD.

Words by M. A. KIDDER.

Music by W. A. OGDEN.

1. O-pen the door for the children, Ten-der-ly gather them in,

2. O-pen the door for the children, See! they are coming in throngs;

3. O-pen the door for the children, Take the dear lambs by the hand;

In from the highways and hedges, In from the pla-ces of sin.

Bid them sit down to the banquet, Teach them your beau-ti-ful songs.

Point them to truth and to Je-sus, Point them to heaven's bright land.

Some are so young and so helpless, Some are so hungry and cold;

Pray you the Father to bless them, Pray you that grace may be given;

Some are so young and so helpless, Some are so hungry and cold;

Open the door for the children, Gather them in - to the fold.

Open the door for the children, "Of such is the kingdom of heaven."

Open the door for the children, Gather them in - to the fold.

Chorus.

Gather them in, oh, gather them in, Gather, oh, gather them in;

Gather them in, oh, gather them in, Gather, oh, gather them in;

Gath - - er them in, Gath - - er them in;

Gather them in, oh, gather them in, Gather, oh, gather them in;

Open the door for the children, Gather them in - to the fold.

Open the door for the children, Gather them in - to the fold.

Open the door for the children, Gather them in - to the. fold.

GOLDEN GLEAMS.

Words by Mrs. M. A. KIDDER.

W. H. DOANE.

1. When I'm dreaming, sad-ly dreaming, Of the tri - als here be - low,

2. When I'm dreaming, soft-ly dreaming, Of the ci - ty of the blest,

3. When I'm dreaming, sweetly dreaming, Of the pure ce - les - tial land;

Of the dark and sore tempta - tions, Ev'-ry hu - man heart must know;

Where the wick-ed cease from troubling, And the wea - ry are at rest:

Of the crowns and spotless garments, And the ho - ly an - gel band;

While I dread each surging bil - low, As a - round my soul they foam,

While I hear sweet Calvary's sto - ry, Chanted on the heavenly hills,

When I near sweet heaven's por - tal, Oh, what glo - ries meet my sight!

Gold-en gleams shine on my pil - low From the land without a storm.

Gold-en gleams from Je - sus' glo - ry, All my long - ing spirit fills.

Gold-en gleams of joys im - mor - tal, Where King Je - sus is the light.

Heavenly ci - ty, bless-ed mansion, When I catch thy gold - en gleams,

Heavenly ci - ty, bless-ed mansion, When I catch thy gold - en gleams,

How it soothes my ach - ing spir - it— How it gilds my earth - ly dreams.

How it soothes my ach - ing spir - it— How it gilds my earth - ly dreams.

LITTLE SONG.

Steady movement, nearly as in 4—4 time.

1st. Time.

1. { Lit - tle star with twinkling eye, God has placed thee in the sky;
     Lit - tle bird with gold- en wing, God has taught thee . . . . . .
D. C. Float - ing in the summer air, God . has made your . . . . . .

2. { Lit - tle, mer - ry, laughing child, Ev - er play - ful, ev - er wild,
     Full of glad- ness, full of love, God has made thee, ...
D. C. When thy life on earth is past, He will take thee . . . . . .

2d Time.

D. C.

how to sing; Little clouds that lightly rest On the bosom of the west,
form so fair.

D. C.

God a - bove; He thy happy spir- it keeps, For he nev - er, nev- er sleeps;
home at last.

HOW CAN I KEEP FROM SINGING.

Rev. R. LOWRY.
From "Bright Jewels," by per.

1. My life flows on in end - less song; A-bove earth's la - men - ta- tion, I

2. What tho' my joys and comfort die? The Lord my Saviour liv- eth; What

3. I lift my eyes; the cloud grows thin; I see the blue a - bove it; And

catch the sweet, tho' far - off hymn That hails a new cre - a - tion;

tho' the dark - ness gath - er round? Songs in the night He giv - eth;

day by day this path - way smooths, Since first I learned to love it;

Through all the tu - mult and the strife, I hear the mu - sic ring- ing; It

No storm can shake my inmost calm, While to that re - fuge clinging; Since

The peace of Christ makes fresh my heart, A fountain ev - er springing; All

finds an ech - o in my soul— How can I keep from singing?

Christ is Lord of heav'n and earth, How can I keep from singing?

things are mine since I am His— How can I keep from singing?

LET ME GO. 8s & 7s.

W. B. BRADBURY.

1. Let me go where saints are go - ing, To the man-sions of the blest,

2. Let me go where none are wea - ry, Where is raised no wail of woe.
3. Let me go, why should I tar - ry? What has earth to bind me here?

Chorus. Let me go, 'tis Je - sus calls me, Let me gain the realms of day,

Fine.

Let me go where my Re-deem - er Has prepared his peo - ple's rest.

Fine.

Let me go and bathe my spir - it, In the rap - tures an - gels know.
What but cares and toils and sor-rows? What but death and pain and fear?

Bear me o - ver, an - gel pin-ions, Longs my soul to be a - way.

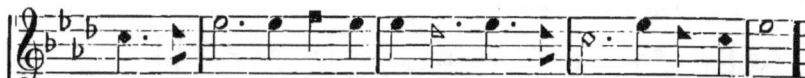

I would gain the realms of brightness, Where they dwell for ev-er-more,

Let me go, for bliss e-ter nal, Lures my soul a-way, a-way,
Let me go, for hopes most cherished, Blas-ted round me of-ten lie

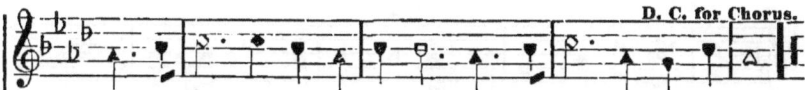

D. C. for Chorus.

I would join the friends that wait me, Ov-er on the oth-er shore.

D. C.

And the vic-tor's song tri-umphant, Thrills my heart, I can-not stay.
O! I've gather-ed brightest flow-ers, But to see them fade and die.

"'TIS I! BE NOT AFRAID."

From "Pure Gold," By per.

J. H. TENNY.

1. Toss'd with rough winds, and faint with fear, A - bove the tem - pest, soft and clear,

2. These rag - ing winds, this surg - ing sea, Bear not a breath of wrath to thee:

3. Mine eyes are watching by thy bed, Mine arms are un - der-neath thy head,

4. When on the oth - er side, thy feet Shall rest where welcome thou-sands meet;

What still, small ac - cents greet mine ear? 'Tis I! be not a - fraid!

That storm has all been spent on me'; 'Tis I! be not a - fraid!

My bless - ing is a - round thee shed; 'Tis I! be not a - fraid!

One well-known voice thy heart shall greet; 'Tis I! be not a - fraid!

Chorus.
'Tis I! 'Tis I! be not a - fraid, 'Tis
'Tis I!
'Tis I! 'Tis I! 'Tis I! be not a - fraid, 'Tis
'Tis I! 'Tis I!
I! thy Lord, thy Life, thy Light, 'Tis I! be not a - fraid!
I! thy Lord, thy Life, thy Light, 'Tis I! be not a - fraid!

AWAY! AWAY!

W. B. Bradbury.

1. A - way! a - way! not a mo - ment to lin - ger, Haste we now with
2. A - way! a - way! where the an - gels are bend - ing Light - ly o'er the

3. A - way! a - way! for the mo-ments are fly - ing, Time for us will

4. A - way! a - way! not a mo - ment to lin - ger, Haste we now with

foot-step free, Where those who love in the vineyard to labor, Wait for you and me.
house of prayer, Glad hymns of praise to the Lord of the Sabbath, Sweetly echo there.

soon be o'er; This holy day we will try to improve it, Ere its light is o'er.

footstep free, Where those who love in the vineyard to labor, Wait for you and me

Chorus.

To the Sun-day-School re-joic-ing we will go, 'Tis a place where all are

To the Sun-day-School re-joic-ing we will go, 'Tis a place where all are

happy here below, Where the way of life we learn to know, And seek our home a-bove.

happy here below, Where the way of life we learn to know, And seek our home a-bove.

CHANT. "JUST AS I AM."

1. Just as I am, with- | out one | plea, | But that thy blood was | shed for | me,
2. Just as I am, and | waiting | not | To rid my soul of | one dark | blot;
3. Just as I am, though | tossed a- | bout | With many a conflict, | many a | doubt,
4. To Father, Son, and | Ho - ly | Ghost, | The God, whom earth and | heav'n a- | dore,

And that thou bidst me | come to | Thee, | O Lamb of | God, I | come.
To Thee, whose blood can | cleanse each | spot, | O Lamb of | God, I | come.
With fears within, and | fears with, | out, | O Lamb of | God, I | come.
Be glory as it | was, is | now | and shall be | ever | more. | A- | men.

IS THERE ONE FOR ME?

T. F. SEWARD.

1. Mansions are prepared a - bove, By the gracious God of love; Many will those

2. Crowns that dazzle human eye, Wait for those who reach the sky; Many will those

mansions see—Is there one prepared for me? Is there one for me? Is there one for

bright crowns be? Is there one prepared for me? Is there one for me? Is there one for

me? Many will those mansions see— Is there one pre - pared for me?

me? Many will those mansions see— Is there one pre - pared for me?

3. Robes of spotless white are given,
  By the glorious King of Heaven;
  All can have them, they are free,—
  Is there one prepared for me?—*Chorus.*

4. Harps of solemn sound above,
  Swell loud praises to His love;
  Oh! how sweet their sounds will be,—
  Is there one prepared for me?—*Chorus.*

EVEN ME.

W. B. Bradbury.

Steady movement, nearly as to 4 -4 time.

·1. Lord, I hear of show'rs of blessings, Thou art scatt'ring full and free; Show'rs the thirsty land
[refreshing;

2. Pass me not, O God, my Father, Sinful though my heart may be; Thou might'st leave me, but the
[rather

3. Pass me not, O gracious Saviour, Let me live and cling to thee; Fain I'm longing for thy favor;
4. Pass me not, O mighty Spirit, Thou canst make the blind to see; Witnesses of   Jesus' merit,

Let some droppings fall on me.   E - ven me,   E - ven me, Let some droppings fall on me.

Let thy   mercy   fall on   me.   E - ven me,   E - ven me, Let some droppings fall on me.

Whilst thou'rt calling, call on me.   E - ven me,   E - ven me, Let some droppings fall on me.
Speak the word of power to me.   E - ven me,   E - ven me, Let some droppings fall on me.

A- - - - - - - - - men.

1 O turn ye, O turn ye, for why will you die,
   When God in great mercy is | coming..so | nigh?
   Now Jesus invites you, the Spirit says, come,
   And angels are waiting to | welcome..you | home.

2 How vain the delusion, that while you delay,
   Your hearts may grow better by | staying..a- | way;
   Come wretched, come starving, come just as you be,
   While streams of salvation are | flowing..so | free.

3 And now Christ is ready your souls to receive;
   O how can you question, if | you will..be- | lieve?
   If sin is your burden, why will you not come?
   'Tis you he bids welcome; he | bids you..come | home.

4 In riches, in pleasure, what can you obtain,
   To soothe your affliction, or | banish..your | pain?
   To bear up your spirit when summon'd to die,
   Or waft you to mansions of | glory..on | high?   A-men.

CHANT.

1 Sinners, will you scorn the message,
    Sent in mercy | from..a- | bove?
Every sentence—O, how tender !
    Every line is | full..of | love ;
        Listen to it—
    Every line is | full..of | love.

2 Hear the heralds of the Gospel,
    News from Zion's | king..pro- | claim,
To each rebel sinner—' Pardon,
    Free forgiveness | in..his | name !'
        How important!
    Free forgiveness | in..his | name !

3 O, ye angels, hovering round us,
    Waiting spirits, | speed..your | way,
Hasten to the court of heaven,
    Tidings bear with- | out..de- | lay ;
        Rebel sinners
    Glad the message | will..o- | bey.

————

1 Descend, celestial Dove,
    And make thy | pres..ence | known ;
Reveal our Saviour's love,
    And seal us | for..thine | own !
Unblest by thee, our works are vain ;
Nor can we e'er ac- | cep..tance | gain.

2 When our incarnate God,
    The sovereign | Prince..of | light,
In Jordan's swelling flood
    Received the | ho..ly | rite,
In open view thy form come down,
And, dove-like, flew the | King..to | crown.

O GIVE THANKS. Chant.

Psalm 136.

WM. B. BRADBURY.

1. O give thanks unto the Lord; for he is good: for his mercy endureth for - ev-er.

3. O give thanks to the Lord of lords: for his mercy endureth for - ev-er.

5. To him that by wisdom made the heavens: for his mercy endureth for - ev-er.
7. To him that made great lights: for his mercy endureth for - ev-er.

9. Who remembered us in our low estate: for his mercy endureth for - ev-er.
11. Who giveth food to all flesh: for his mercy endureth for - ev-er.

2. O give thanks unto the God of gods: for his mercy endureth for-ev-er.

4. To him who alone doeth great wonders: for his mercy endureth for-ev-er.

6. To him that stretched out the earth
above the waters: for his mercy endureth for-ev-er.
8. The sun to rule by day; the moon
and stars to rule by night: for his mercy endureth for-ev-er.

10. And hath redeemed us from our enemies: for his mercy endureth forever.
12. O give thanks unto the God of heaven: for his mercy endureth forever.   Amen.

COME UNTO ME. Chant.

Wm. B. Bradbury.

1. With tearful eyes I look around, Life seems a dark and storm - y sea:

2. It tells me of a place of rest— It tells me where my soul may flee;

3. When nature shudders, loth to part From all I love, en - joy, and see,

4. Come, for all else must fall and die; Earth is no resting - place for thee;
5. O voice of mercy! voice of love! In conflict, grief, and ag - o - ny,

Yet, 'midst the gloom, I hear a sound, A heavenly whis - per, Come to me.

Oh! to the weary, faint, opprest, How sweet the bid - ding, Come to me.

When a faint chill steals o'er my heart, A sweet voice ut - ters, Come to me.

Heavenward direct thy weeping eye: I am thy por - tion, Come to me.
Support me, cheer me from above, And gently whis - per, Come to me.

GREGORIAN.

1. Our Father, who art in heaven,   hallowed be   thy   name:

2. Give us this   day   our dai - ly   bread,

3. And lead us not into temptation, but de-   liv - er   us   from   evil:

Thy kingdom come, thy will be done on   earth, as it is   in   heaven;

And forgive us our trespasses, as we forgive   them   that trespass a-gainst us.

For thine is the kingdom, the power, and the   glory, for - ever. A - men.

LIGHT AND COMFORT.

W. B. BRADBURY.

1. Light and com - fort of my soul, When the bil - lows o'er me roll;

2. Lord, my soul in tears would mourn, All the an - guish thou hast borne;

3. Mocked and scourged, condemned to die, On the cross ex - tend - ed high;

Thou dost bid me in thy word, Cast my bur - den on the Lord,

In the gar - den I would be, Lone - ly watch - er still with thee.

Ten - ant of the lone - ly tomb, Might-y conqueror o'er its gloom,

Je - sus, Sa - viour, once betrayed, Sac - ri - fice for sin - ners made;

Thou hast suffered, thou hast bled, Thorns have pierced thy sacred head;

Crown'd vic - to - rious God of love, To thy Fa-ther's home a - bove,

Wretched, lost, to thee I fly, Save, oh, save me, or I die.

Je - sus, while I cling to thee, Let thy sor - row plead for me.

Grant my soul a place at last, Where the storms of life are past.

INDEX FOR CRYSTAL GEMS.

J. M. ARMSTRONG, MUSIC TYPOGRAPHER, N. E. COR. CHESTNUT & FIFTH STS., PHILADELPHIA.